D1522060

THE CENOZOIC ERA
AGE OF
MAMMALS

THE GEOLOGIC HISTORY OF EARTH

THE CENOZOIC ERA
AGE OF
MAMMALS

EDITED BY JOHN P. RAFFERTY, ASSOCIATE EDITOR, EARTH SCIENCES

Britannica®
Educational Publishing

IN ASSOCIATION WITH

ROSEN
EDUCATIONAL SERVICES

Published in 2011 by Britannica Educational Publishing
(a trademark of Encyclopædia Britannica, Inc.)
in association with Rosen Educational Services, LLC
29 East 21st Street, New York, NY 10010

First Edition

Britannica Educational Publishing
Michael I. Levy: Executive Editor
J.E. Luebering: Senior Manager
Marilyn L. Barton: Senior Coordinator, Production Control
Steven Bosco: Director, Editorial Technologies
Lisa S. Braucher: Senior Producer and Data Editor
Yvette Charboneau: Senior Copy Editor
Kathy Nakamura: Manager, Media Acquisition
John P. Rafferty: Associate Editor, Earth Sciences

Rosen Educational Services
Heather M. Moore Niver: Rosen Editor
Nelson Sá: Designer
Cindy Reiman: Photography Manager
Matthew Cauli: Designer, Cover Design
Introduction by Cathy Vanderhoof

Library of Congress Cataloging-in-Publication Data

The Cenozoic era : age of mammals / edited by John P. Rafferty.
    p. cm. — (The geologic history of Earth)
In association with Britannica Educational Publishing, Rosen Educational Services
Includes bibliographical references and index.
ISBN 978-1-61530-144-7 (lib. bdg.)
1. Geology, Stratigraphic—Cenozoic. 2. Paleoecology—Cenozoic. 3. Paleontology—Cenozoic. I. Rafferty, John P.
QE690.C416 2011
560'.178—dc22

                                                                    2010010471

Manufactured in the United States of America

On the cover: Extinction of the rapacious reptile transformed Earth's population as the mammal flourished throughout the Cenozoic era. *Manoj Shah/Stone/Getty Images*

On page 12: The Mississippi River is associated with large marine delta deposits of Quaternary age. *James L. Stanfield/National Geographic/Getty Images*

On pages 5, 21, 30 73, 104, 127, 163, 201, 231, 232, 234, and 236: "Lucy," the most famous *Australopithecus* fossil specimen, dates back to the Late Pliocene Epoch. *Dave Einsel/Getty Images*

CONTENTS

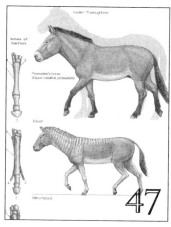

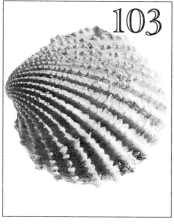

moth   African savanna elephant

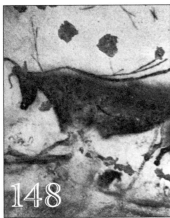

INTRODUCTION

Woolly mammoths, sabre-toothed tigers, ice ages covering the Earth, the formation of the Grand Canyon—and us! All are part of the third major era in Earth's history, known as the Cenozoic era, or era of modern life. Beginning after the great extinction of the dinosaurs, which ended the Mesozoic Era, and continuing to life today, this book provides a lively journey through the Cenozoic Era: the latest chapter in our planet's continuing story of evolution and change.

The Cenozoic Era began about 65.5 million years ago, at a time when Earth's climate was warm, sea levels were high, and reptiles were the dominant life-forms on Earth. During the ensuing millions of years, mammals became most prominent, humans evolved, plant life diversified, and sharply differentiated climate zones became the norm. The Cenozoic also saw the formation of many of Earth's great mountain ranges, including the Alps, Himalayas, and Rocky Mountains of the American West.

Nineteenth-century geologists divided the Cenozoic into two major subdivisions: the Tertiary, spanning the interval from the beginning of the Cenozoic Era to the base of the Pleistocene Epoch, and the Quaternary, from the onset of the Pleistocene Epoch to the present. Scientists now agree on dividing the era into three major periods, splitting the traditional Tertiary Period into the Paleogene (65.5 million to 23 million years ago) and the Neogene (23 million to 2.6 million years ago). Each period is divided into several smaller intervals. The Paleogene Period is made up of the Paleocene Epoch, from 65.5 million to 55.8 million years ago, the Eocene, from 55.8 to 33.9 million years ago, and the Oligocene, from 33.9 to 23 million years ago. The Neogene encompasses the Miocene epoch, from 23 million to 5.3 million years ago and the Pliocene, from 5.3 to 2.6 million years ago. The third period, still known as the Quaternary, is divided into the Pleistocene Epoch, from 2.6 million to 11,700 years ago, and the Holocene, from 11,700 years ago to the present.

The early Tertiary, or Paleogene, Period was one of the warmest periods in Earth's history, with little temperature difference between the polar regions and the equator. Life in the oceans had been decimated by the K-T mass extinction event, at the end of the Cretaceous Period. This was accompanied by the disappearance of the dinosaurs on land. During the next 10 million years, from the beginning of the Paleocene to the beginning of the Eocene Epoch, more than 20 orders of mammals rapidly evolved to fill this gap, along with a variety of large flightless birds. An extinction event near the end of the Paleocene Period replaced some earlier mammalian species with ancestors of many of the animals we know today. Mammals such as primitive horses, deer, rodents, hares, and early primates all appeared during the Eocene Epoch.

The boundary between the Paleocene and Eocene was marked by a short period of warming, known as the Paleocene-Eocene Thermal Maximum, before the onset of a rapid drop in average global temperature and the beginning of the long, cool interval that continues through today. These dramatic climate changes in large part result from the movement of continental landmasses into a configuration close to their present-day locations, causing significant changes in ocean currents and weather patterns. Some major continental developments of the early Cenozoic Era include the separation of Australia from Antarctica and the collision of India and southern Asia. The locations of global landmasses also affected the spread of mammals between the continents, with land bridges appearing and disappearing according to sea-level changes and continental shift multiple times during the Cenozoic Era.

The Eocene Epoch saw the emergence of the first marine mammals: cetaceans, including whales, porpoises, and dolphins; and sirenians, related to modern manatees. Primates evolved and diversified in many areas of the world, with the emergence of lemurs as well as ancestors of modern monkeys and apes. The Eocene Epoch also ushered in the first ancestors of elephants and bats and the first examples of many other modern mammalian orders, and thus earned the epoch its name, which is derived from the Greek word *eos*, or "dawn."

The Paleogene Period ends with the Oligocene Epoch, an interval characterized by a relatively temperate global climate and favourable conditions for the spread and diversification of many life-forms introduced in the earlier Paleogenic epochs. Fossils of the largest land mammal of all time, a sort of giant hornless rhinoceros belonging to the genus *Indricotherium*, have been identified from this period in Asia, and ape and monkey fossils are found in both Egypt and South America. Another significant event of the Oligocene Epoch was the separation of South America, which led to the evolution of mammalian species in isolation from the rest of the Western Hemisphere.

Although the break between the Paleogene and Neogene Periods was not heralded by a dramatic extinction event, it was marked by a change in the fossil record. By the beginning of the Miocene Epoch, many archaic mammalian groups had disappeared, and most life-forms from this period closely resemble their modern relatives. Fossil records from the Miocene exist throughout the world, offering scientists a complete view of life during this period. Half of the mammalian families of modern times existed in the Miocene as well. This period also saw a wave of mammalian migration across land bridges connecting the continents of Europe, Asia, North America, and Africa. Horses continued to evolve in North America, while bear-dogs, rhinoceroses, weasels, and a variety of deerlike animals appeared in Eurasia. Mastodons, mammoths, and other relatives of modern elephants spread from Africa into Europe. Climatic cooling and drying led to the expansion of grassland ecosystems and the development of a variety of grazing mammals. Only South America and Australia continued to be separated from the other landmasses, leading to the evolution of species unique to those regions. The Miocene Epoch was also a crucial time for primate evolution, with the development of a primate group known as dryopithecines, from which modern apes and humans most likely originated.

Primate evolution continued during the Pliocene Epoch, the second major division of the Neogene Period. Appearing during this time period are the first examples of *Ardipithecus* and *Australopithecus*, a group of extinct creatures closely related to, if not actually ancestors of, modern human beings. Like humans, they walked on two legs but had small brains more similar to apes. The most famous fossil specimen of *Australopithecus* is "Lucy," found in southern Africa and dating from 3.2 million years ago during the Late Pliocene Epoch. However, an older fossil called "Ardi," belonging to the species *Ardipithecus ramidus* was recently dated to 4.4 million years ago. Some scientists believe that *Ardipithecus ramidus* is the oldest-known direct human ancestor. In the Western Hemisphere, the land connection between North and South America was re-established in the mid-Pliocene, allowing sundry terrestrial animals such as opossums, sloths, and porcupines to migrate from South America into the North American continent.

The third major division of the Cenozoic Era is the Quaternary Period, whose starting date of 2,588,000 million years ago is based on geologic evidence of widespread expansion of ice sheets across the northern continents. In fact, the Pleistocene Epoch, which begins the Quaternary Period, is characterized by a repeated series of glacial advances and retreats and is sometimes known as the Great Ice Age. This period was not uniformly cold and ice covered, however. Studies of deep-sea sediments now suggest that the Pleistocene consisted of four or five major glacial expansions, separated by interglacial stages with climates generally similar to those of today. During times of extensive glaciation, up to 30 percent of Earth's land area was covered by glaciers, and ice sheets extended over many portions of the northern oceans. Most glacial ice was located in the Northern Hemisphere, where ice sheets extended as far as southern Illinois in North America and covered most of Great Britain, Germany, Poland, and Russia in Eurasia. Smaller glaciers and ice caps appeared in high altitudes in the Andes, in New Zealand, and on the mountains of Africa. Even areas that were not ice covered experienced significantly lower temperatures, a zone of permafrost sometimes present for hundreds of kilometres around the glacier margins.

As the glaciers moved across the land and down from the mountaintops, the large ice sheets stripped top layers of soil and deposited the glacial sediment along the margins, creating some of the richest agricultural regions in the world. In mountainous terrain the glaciers carved out valleys and left towering peaks where the underlying rock was harder. The movement of the glaciers also created large lakes, sometimes by scouring out deep basins, as was the case with the Great Lakes of North America; but climatic changes and the opening and closing of glacial outlets also reshaped the land. The Great Salt Lake in Utah as well as the Dead Sea in Israel are both remnants of much larger Pleistocene lakes caused by large amounts of precipitation as the glacial cover changed the atmospheric flow and created new weather patterns. Changing levels of glaciation also dramatically affected sea level with many areas of the continental shelf exposed as dry land.

These dramatic climate and habitat shifts created evolutionary pressure for both animals and plants. Although most Pleistocene animals are clearly related to species alive today, they were uniquely suited to the environments in which they lived. Some species, such as the woolly mammoth and woolly rhinoceros, were clearly adapted to the colder conditions with their thick fur. It was also a time of gigantism in many terrestrial mammals, for reasons that are not completely understood. Pleistocene mammals included the giant beaver, giant sloth, stag-moose, and cave bear, as well as the giant mastodon, all of which are now extinct. The reason for their demise is a subject of debate among scientists. One theory suggests that the disappearance of some Pleistocene species may be the first example of extinction resulting from human interaction in the form of overhunting. There is little compelling evidence to support this idea, however, and the effects of climate and habitat change are the more likely causes.

The habitat changes that followed fluctuations in Earth's climate during the Pleistocene were also factors in the evolution of modern hominids. The shift from forests to drier grasslands in Africa favoured an upright stance and the ability to run and walk long distances, thus freeing the hands to grasp and eventually use tools. The genus *Homo*, to which modern humans belong, appeared approximately 2 million years ago in Africa. Fossil examples of *Homo erectus* exist from Africa, Europe, and Asia during the early Pleistocene, followed by Neanderthals, other human relatives, and human beings (*Homo sapiens*) themselves as the epoch went on. By about 30,000 years ago, Neanderthals had disappeared, and modern humans had spread across all the continents except Antarctica.

The current period of geologic history is known as the Holocene Epoch and designates the period of Earth's existence dominated by human influence, beginning a mere 11,700 years ago. During this short period, Earth has enjoyed relatively stable, cool conditions, as compared to most of the planet's history. This favourable climate allowed for widespread agriculture and the development of human civilizations throughout the world. Even as early as the Bronze Age, approximately 3000 BC, we can see geologic evidence of human activities on the environment, as European communities began to cut down forests for charcoal and allow the use of the land for farming, which caused soil erosion on the hillsides and created anthropogenic sediment on the floodplains. Farming, deforestation, and more recently industrial activity by humans has continued to affect Earth's environment, leading to a concern that we may be entering a new period of climatic change.

CHAPTER 1
AN OVERVIEW OF CENOZOIC TIME

The Cenozoic is the youngest and most recent of Earth's geologic eras. Emerging from a time of mass extinction, Cenozoic animals diversified, filling the empty niches previously occupied by the dinosaurs. The era was characterized by the radiation of mammals, the proliferation of grasses across the planet, and the migration of continents to their present location. The Cenozoic was also known as the time in which the Indian subcontinent crashed into southern Asia, forming the Himalayas, and land bridges connecting the continents rose and fell with changing climatic conditions and tectonic activity.

Near the end of the era, great ice sheets expanded and contracted over the northern continents. Antarctica, a landmass once lush with vegetation and a rich diversity of animal life, froze over shortly after its exile at the bottom of the world. The Cenozoic Era was the setting in which the primates arose. Some groups of primates remained quadrupedal and arboreal, whereas others developed bipedal locomotion and engaged in tool use. The most notable of the latter type was the genus *Homo*, whose members created increasingly sophisticated tools that they used to dominate the Earth.

The term Cenozoic, originally spelled Kainozoic, was introduced by John Phillips in an 1840 *Penny Cyclopaedia* article to designate the most recent of the three major subdivisions of the Phanerozoic. Derived from the Greek for "recent life," it reflects the sequential development

GEOLOGIC TIME SCALE

Left vertical scale: present — Cenozoic Era — Mesozoic Era — Paleozoic Era — Precambrian time. 1,000[1] · 2,000[1] · 3,000[1] · 4,000[1] · 4,600[1]

Eonothem/Eon	Erathem/Era	System/Period	Series/Epoch	Stage/Age	mya[1]
Phanerozoic	Cenozoic	Quaternary	Holocene		0.0117
			Pleistocene	Tarantian	0.126
				"Ionian"	0.781
				Calabrian	1.806
				Gelasian	2.588
		Neogene	Pliocene	Piacenzian	3.600
				Zanclean	5.332
			Miocene	Messinian	7.246
				Tortonian	11.608
				Serravallian	13.82
				Langhian	15.97
				Burdigalian	20.43
				Aquitanian	23.03
		Paleogene	Oligocene	Chattian	28.4 ± 0.1
				Rupelian	33.9 ± 0.1
			Eocene	Priabonian	37.2 ± 0.1
				Bartonian	40.4 ± 0.2
				Lutetian	48.6 ± 0.2
				Ypresian	55.8 ± 0.2
			Paleocene	Thanetian	58.7 ± 0.2
				Selandian	~61.1
				Danian	65.5 ± 0.3
	Mesozoic	Cretaceous	Upper	Maastrichtian	70.6 ± 0.6
				Campanian	83.5 ± 0.7
				Santonian	85.8 ± 0.7
				Coniacian	~88.6
				Turonian	93.6 ± 0.8
				Cenomanian	99.6 ± 0.9
			Lower	Albian	112.0 ± 1.0
				Aptian	125.0 ± 1.0
				Barremian	130.0 ± 1.5
				Hauterivian	~133.9
				Valanginian	140.2 ± 3.0
				Berriasian	145.5 ± 4.0

Eonothem/Eon	Erathem/Era	System/Period	Series/Epoch	Stage/Age	mya[1]
Phanerozoic	Mesozoic	Jurassic	Upper	Tithonian	145.5 ± 4.0
				Kimmeridgian	150.8 ± 4.0
				Oxfordian	~155.6
			Middle	Callovian	161.2 ± 4.0
				Bathonian	164.7 ± 4.0
				Bajocian	167.7 ± 3.5
				Aalenian	171.6 ± 3.0
			Lower	Toarcian	175.6 ± 2.0
				Pliensbachian	183.0 ± 1.5
				Sinemurian	189.6 ± 1.5
				Hettangian	196.5 ± 1.0
		Triassic	Upper	Rhaetian	199.6 ± 0.6
				Norian	203.6 ± 1.5
				Carnian	216.5 ± 2.0
			Middle	Ladinian	~228.7
				Anisian	237.0 ± 2.0
			Lower	Olenekian	~245.9
				Induan	~249.5
	Paleozoic	Permian	Lopingian		251.0 ± 0.4
				Changhsingian	253.8 ± 0.7
				Wuchiapingian	260.4 ± 0.7
			Guadalupian	Capitanian	265.8 ± 0.7
				Wordian	268.0 ± 0.7
				Roadian	270.6 ± 0.7
			Cisuralian	Kungurian	275.6 ± 0.7
				Artinskian	284.4 ± 0.7
				Sakmarian	294.6 ± 0.8
				Asselian	299.0 ± 0.8
		Carboniferous	Pennsylvanian[2] Upper	Gzhelian	303.4 ± 0.9
				Kasimovian	307.2 ± 1.0
			Middle	Moscovian	311.7 ± 1.1
			Lower	Bashkirian	318.1 ± 1.3
			Mississippian[2] Upper	Serpukhovian	328.3 ± 1.6
			Middle	Visean	345.3 ± 2.1
			Lower	Tournaisian	359.2 ± 2.5

[1] Millions of years ago.

[2] Both the Mississippian and Pennsylvanian time units are formally designated as sub-periods within the Carboniferous Period.

[3] Several Cambrian unit age boundaries are informal and are awaiting ratified definitions.

Encyclopædia Britannica, Inc. Source: International Commission on Stratigraphy (ICS)

Eonothem/Eon	Erathem/Era	System/Period	Series/Epoch	Stage/Age	mya[1]
Phanerozoic	Paleozoic	Devonian	Upper	Famennian	359.2 ± 2.5
					374.5 ± 2.6
				Frasnian	385.3 ± 2.6
			Middle	Givetian	391.8 ± 2.7
				Eifelian	397.5 ± 2.7
			Lower	Emsian	407.0 ± 2.8
				Pragian	411.2 ± 2.8
				Lochkovian	416.0 ± 2.8
		Silurian	Pridoli		418.7 ± 2.7
			Ludlow	Ludfordian	421.3 ± 2.6
				Gorstian	422.9 ± 2.5
			Wenlock	Homerian	426.2 ± 2.4
				Sheinwoodian	428.2 ± 2.3
			Llandovery	Telychian	436.0 ± 1.9
				Aeronian	439.0 ± 1.8
				Rhuddanian	443.7 ± 1.5
		Ordovician	Upper	Hirnantian	445.6 ± 1.5
				Katian	455.8 ± 1.6
				Sandbian	460.9 ± 1.6
			Middle	Darriwilian	468.1 ± 1.6
				Dapingian	471.8 ± 1.6
			Lower	Floian	478.6 ± 1.7
				Tremadocian	488.3 ± 1.7
		Cambrian[3]	Furongian	Stage 10	~492.0
				Stage 9	~496.0
				Paibian	~499.0
			Series 3	Guzhangian	~503.0
				Drumian	~506.5
				Stage 5	~510.0
			Series 2	Stage 4	~515.0
				Stage 3	~521.0
			Terreneuvian	Stage 2	~528.0
				Fortunian	542.0 ± 1.0

Eonothem/Eon	Erathem/Era	System/Period	mya[1]
Precambrian	Proterozoic	Neoproterozoic	Ediacaran — 542
			~635
			Cryogenian — 850
			Tonian — 1,000
		Mesoproterozoic	Stenian — 1,200
			Ectasian — 1,400
			Calymmian — 1,600
		Paleoproterozoic	Statherian — 1,800
			Orosirian — 2,050
			Rhyacian — 2,300
			Siderian — 2,500
	Archean	Neoarchean	2,800
		Mesoarchean	3,200
		Paleoarchean	3,600
		Eoarchean	4,000
		Hadean (informal)	4,600

and diversification of life on Earth from the Paleozoic (ancient life) through the Mesozoic (middle life). Today, the Cenozoic is internationally accepted as the youngest of the three subdivisions of the fossiliferous part of Earth history.

The Cenozoic Era is generally divided into the Paleogene (65.5 million to 23 million years ago), Neogene (23 million to 2.6 million years ago), and Quaternary (2.6 million years ago to the present) periods, the era's traditional division is into the Tertiary and Quaternary periods. The designations Tertiary and Quaternary, however, are relics of early attempts in the late 18th century at formulating a stratigraphic classification that included the now wholly obsolete terms Primary and Secondary. In 1856 Moritz Hörnes introduced the terms Paleogene and Neogene, the latter encompassing rocks equivalent to those described by Charles Lyell as Miocene and older and newer Pliocene (including what he later called the Pleistocene). Subsequent investigators have determined that the designation Neogene correctly applies to the rock systems and corresponding time intervals delineated by Lyell, but some authorities prefer to exclude the Pleistocene from the Neogene. The Paleogene encompasses the Paleocene, Eocene, and Oligocene epochs. (The terms Paleocene and Oligocene were coined subsequent to Lyell's work and inserted in the lower part of the Cenozoic stratigraphic scheme.) The Neogene spans the Miocene and Pliocene epochs, and the Quaternary includes the Pleistocene and Holocene epochs.

GEOLOGIC PROCESSES

Cenozoic rocks are extensively developed on all the continents, particularly on lowland plains, such as the Gulf and

Atlantic coastal plains of North America. They are generally less consolidated than older rocks, but some are indurated (cemented) as a result of high pressure caused by deep burial, chemical diagenesis, or high temperature—namely, metamorphism. Sedimentary rocks predominate during the Cenozoic, and more than half the world's petroleum occurs in such rocks of this age. Igneous rocks are represented by extensive early Cenozoic flood basalts (those of East Greenland and the Deccan trap of India) and the late Cenozoic flood basalts of the Columbia River in Washington, as well as by numerous volcanoes in the circum-Pacific System and ocean island chains such as Hawaii.

Medial moraine of Gornergletscher (Gorner Glacier) in the Pennine Alps near Zermatt, Switz. Jerome Wyckoff

Several of the world's great mountain ranges were built during the Cenozoic. The main Alpine orogeny, which produced the Alps and Carpathians in southern Europe and the Atlas Mountains in northwestern Africa, began roughly between 37 and 24 million years ago. The Himalayas were formed some time after the Indian Plate collided with the Eurasian Plate. These lofty mountains marked the culmination of the great uplift that occurred during the late Cenozoic when the Indian Plate drove many hundreds of kilometres into the underbelly of Asia. They are the product of the low-angle underthrusting of the northern edge of the Indian Plate under the southern edge of the Eurasian Plate.

From about five million years ago, the Rocky Mountains and adjoining areas were elevated by rapid uplift of the entire region without faulting. This upwarping sharply steepened stream gradients, enabling rivers to achieve greater erosional power. As a result, deep river valleys and canyons, such as the Grand Canyon, of the Colorado River in northern Arizona, were cut into broad upwarps of sedimentary rock during late Cenozoic time.

On a global scale the Cenozoic witnessed the further dismemberment of the Northern Hemispheric supercontinent of Laurasia: Greenland and Scandinavia separated during the early Cenozoic about 55 million years ago and the Norwegian-Greenland Sea emerged, linking the North Atlantic and Arctic oceans. The Atlantic continued to expand while the Pacific experienced a net reduction in size as a result of continued seafloor spreading. The equatorially situated east–west Tethyan seaway linking the Atlantic and Pacific oceans was modified significantly in the east during the middle Eocene (about 45 million years ago) by the junction of India with Eurasia, and it was severed into two parts by the confluence of Africa, Arabia, and Eurasia during the early Miocene approximately 18 million years ago. The western part of the Tethys evolved into the Mediterranean Sea not long after it had been cut off from the global ocean system about 6 to 5 million years ago and had formed evaporite deposits which reach up to several kilometres in thickness in a land-locked basin that may have resembled Death Valley in present-day California. Antarctica remained centred on the South Pole throughout the Cenozoic, but the northern continents converged in a northward direction.

The global climate was much warmer during the early Cenozoic than it is today, and equatorial-to-polar thermal gradients were less than half of what they are at present. The Earth began to cool about 50 million years ago and, with fluctuations of varying amounts, has continued inexorably to the present interglacial climatic period. It is to be noted that a unique feature of the Cenozoic was the development of glaciation on the Antarctic continent about 35 million years ago and in the Northern Hemisphere between 3 and 2.5 million years ago. Glaciation left an extensive geologic record on the continents in the form of predominantly unconsolidated tills and glacial moraines, which in North America extend in a line as far south as Kansas, Illinois, Ohio, and Long Island, N.Y., and on the ocean floor in the form of ice-rafted detritus dropped from calving icebergs.

CENOZOIC LIFE

Cenozoic life was strikingly different from that of the Mesozoic. The great diversity that characterizes modern-day flora is attributed to the explosive expansion and adaptive radiation of the angiosperms that began during the Late Cretaceous. As climatic differentiation increased over the course of the Cenozoic, flora became more and more provincial. Deciduous angiosperms predominated in colder regions, for example, whereas evergreen varieties prevailed in the subtropics and tropics.

Fauna also underwent dramatic changes during the Cenozoic. The end of the Cretaceous brought the eradication of dinosaurs on land and of large swimming reptiles (such as ichthyosaurs, mosasaurs, and plesiosaurs) in marine environments. Nektonic ammonites, squid-like belemnites, sessile reef-building mollusks known as rudistids, and most microscopic plankton also died out at this time. The Cenozoic witnessed a rapid diversification of life-forms in the ecological niches left vacant by this great terminal Cretaceous extinction. In particular, mammals, having existed for more than 100 million years before the advent of the Cenozoic Era, experienced substantial evolutionary radiation. Marsupials developed a diverse array of adaptive types in Australia and South America, where they were free from the predations of carnivorous placentals. The placental mammals, which today make up more than 95 percent of known mammals, radiated at a rapid rate. Ungulates (hoofed mammals) with clawed feet evolved during the Paleocene (65.5 to about 55.8 million years ago). This epoch saw the development and proliferation of the earliest perissodactyls (odd-toed ungulates, such as horses, tapirs, rhinoceroses, and two extinct groups, the chalicotheres and titanotheres) and artiodactyls (even-toed ungulates, including pigs, peccaries, hippopotamuses, camels, llamas, chevrotains, deer, giraffes, sheep, goats, musk-oxen, antelopes, and cattle). During the later Cenozoic, perissodactyl diversity declined markedly, but artiodactyls continued to diversify. Elephants, which evolved in the late Eocene about 40 million years ago, spread throughout much of the world and underwent tremendous diversification at this time. Many placental forms of giant size, such as the sabre-toothed cat, giant ground sloths, and woolly mammoths, inhabited the forests and the plains in the Pliocene (5.3 to 1.8 million years ago). About this time the first hominids appeared, but early modern humans did not emerge until the Pleistocene.

Among marine life-forms, mollusks (primarily pelecypods and gastropods) became highly diversified, as did reef-building corals characteristic of the tropical belt. Planktonic foraminiferans underwent two major radiations (the first in the Paleocene and the second in the Miocene) punctuated by a long (15- to 20-million-year) mid-Cenozoic reduction in diversity related in all likelihood to global cooling.

Cenozoic life was affected significantly by a major extinction event that occurred between 10,000 and 8,000 years ago. This event, which involved the sudden disappearance of many Ice Age mammals, has been attributed to either of two factors: climatic change following the melting of the most recent Pleistocene glaciers or overkill by Paleolithic hunters. The latter is regarded by many as the more likely cause, as the rapidly improved technology of Paleolithic humans permitted more efficient hunting.

CHAPTER 2
THE TERTIARY PERIOD

The Tertiary Period is an unofficial interval of geologic time lasting from approximately 65.5 million to 2.6 million years ago. It is the traditional name for the first of two periods in the Cenozoic Era (65.5 million years ago to the present). The second is the Quaternary Period (2.6 million years ago to the present). The five principal subdivisions of the Tertiary are called epochs, which from oldest to youngest are the Paleocene (65.5–55.8 million years ago), Eocene (55.8–33.9 million years ago), Oligocene (33.9–23 million years ago), Miocene (23–5.3 million years ago), and Pliocene (5.3–2.6 million years ago). Beginning in the late 20th century, many authorities preferred not to use the terms Tertiary and Quaternary, opting instead to divide the time intervals encompassed by each into two different intervals known as the Paleogene Period (65.5–23 million years ago) and the Neogene Period (which previously spanned the interval between 23 million years ago and the present). In 2005 the International Commission on Stratigraphy (ICS) decided to recommend keeping the Tertiary and Quaternary in their geologic time scale, but only as sub-eras within the Cenozoic. The sub-era structure was abandoned by the ICS in 2008, and the Tertiary Period became officially replaced by the Paleogene and Neogene periods. (At present, the Neogene encompasses the interval between 23 million and 2.6 million years ago.)

The Tertiary was an interval of enormous geologic, climatic, oceanographic, and biological change. It spanned the transition from a globally warm world containing relatively high sea levels and dominated by reptiles to a world of polar glaciation, sharply differentiated climate zones, and mammalian dominance. It began in the aftermath of the mass extinction event that occurred at the very end of the Cretaceous Period (the so-called K–T boundary), when as much as 80 percent of species, including the dinosaurs, disappeared. The Tertiary witnessed the dramatic evolutionary expansion of mammals as well as of flowering plants, insects, birds, corals, deep-sea organisms, marine plankton, and mollusks (especially clams and snails), among many other groups. The Tertiary Period saw huge alterations in Earth's systems and the development of the ecological and climatic conditions that characterize the modern world. The end of the Tertiary is characterized by the growth of glaciers in the Northern Hemisphere and the emergence of primates that later gave rise to modern humans (*Homo sapiens*), chimpanzees (*Pan troglodytes*), and other living great apes.

The name Tertiary was introduced by Italian geologist Giovanni Arduino in 1760. Arduino devised a stratigraphic system in which sedimentary rocks containing fossils were called "tertiary" rocks to distinguish them from igneous and metamorphic rocks present in the cores of mountain ranges ("primary" rocks), the shales and limestones of Europe ("secondary" rocks), and surficial gravel ("quaternary" rocks). Although by modern standards his system appears simplistic, it provides the initial framework on which modern stratigraphy is based.

THE TERTIARY ENVIRONMENT

The configuration of continents and oceans at the beginning of Tertiary times bore some resemblance to that of the present day. At the beginning of the period, the relative positions of North and South America, Europe, Asia, and Africa approximated those of modern times, but all were separated from one another by large seaways. This ocean-continent geometry diverted ocean currents, which were important factors in determining regional climate. Tectonic forces eventually closed off some of these seaways and opened others, such as the one between Australia and Antarctica. Land bridges, such as the one connecting North and South America, redirected ocean currents and allowed plants and animals to migrate into new areas.

PALEOGEOGRAPHY

The present-day configuration of the continents and oceans on Earth is the result of a complex sequence of events involving the growth and rearrangement of Earth's tectonic plates that began almost 200 million years ago. By the beginning of the Tertiary, the supercontinent of Pangea had been fragmenting for more than 100 million years, and the geometry of the continents and oceans had assumed an essentially modern aspect with several notable exceptions. The fragmentation and dispersal of the Southern Hemisphere supercontinent known as Gondwana, which had begun in the early part of the Mesozoic Era (251–65.5 million years ago), continued into the Cenozoic. Australia began to separate from Antarctica about 58 million years ago during the late Paleocene Epoch. The initial subsidence of the South Tasman Rise, which occurred about 35 million years ago during the late Eocene Epoch, resulted in a shallow but inexorably widening oceanic connection between the Indian and Pacific oceans. It was this progressive separation of the two continents that led to the development of the Antarctic Circumpolar Current, a current that sweeps around Antarctica and thermally isolates it from the effects of

MAJOR PALEOGENE PALEOGEOGRAPHIC EVENTS*

AGE	TIME**	PALEOGEOGRAPHIC EVENTS
Middle Oligocene	33–30 mya	Isolation of Antarctica completed after further subsidence of South Tasman Rise.
Early Oligocene	c. 35–33 mya	Tethys severely restricted in the eastern part because of uplift of the Himalayas.
Early Oligocene	37–35 mya	Separation of Greenland and Svalbard and availability of higher-latitude water to North Atlantic.
Early Oligocene	38–35 mya	Shallow connection between the South Pacific and Atlantic developed at Drake Passage.
Eocene-Oligocene Boundary	34–35 mya	Completion of the opening of Labrador Sea that had begun in the Maastrichtian.
Late Eocene	c. 38 mya	Iceland-Faeroe sill sinks below sea level for the first time.
Late Eocene	40–37 mya	Tethys partially restricted north and east of the Indian Plate.
Late Eocene	c. 40 mya	Subsidence of South Tasman Rise permits shallow connection between Indian and Pacific oceans.
Early Eocene	c. 53 mya	Opening Norwegian-Greenland Sea develops surface water exchange with the Arctic Ocean.
Late Eocene and Early Oligocene	37–33 mya	Complete separation of Australia and Antarctica. Australia begins north-ward drift.
Early Paleocene	56–55 mya	Separation of Greenland and Scandinavia and the formation of the Norwegian–Greenland Sea begins.

*Listed are those paleogeographic events that affected global ocean circulation and certain climatic and faunal and floral migration patterns.
**Mya = millions of years ago.

warmer waters and climates to the north. This current was strengthened further and assumed its modern form as Antarctica and South America separated and thus formed the Drake Passage. There is much debate over when this opening actually occurred. Some experts state that the Drake Passage opened as early as during the Eocene about 41 million years ago, whereas others maintain that this event took place as late as the boundary between the Oligocene and Miocene epochs about 23 million years ago.

The collision of India and southern Asia began during the late Paleocene, approximately 55 million years ago, and continues today. The collision produced two main geologic results. First, it began to block the westward-flowing Tethys seaway near the Equator, a process completed with the junction of Africa and Asia near present-day Iran about 18 million years ago. Second, the creation of the

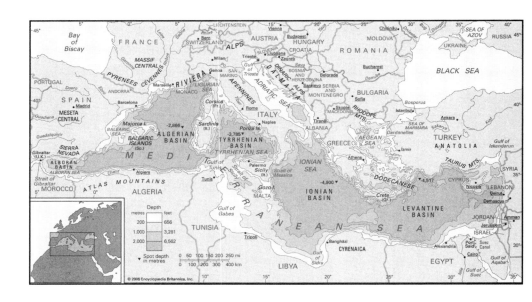

The bathymetry of the Mediterranean Sea.

Himalayas and the Plateau of Tibet, which resulted from the collision, altered global climates by changing patterns of weathering (and thus the transfer rate of carbon to the atmosphere) as well as wind circulation. India's collision with southern Asia also altered patterns of oceanic productivity by increasing erosion and thus nutrient runoff to the Indian Ocean.

The present-day Mediterranean Sea is a geologically recent descendant of a portion of the Tethys seaway. About 5.6 million years ago, during the Messinian Age, the western remnant of the Tethys seaway was subject to a brief paroxysm, known as the Messinian salinity crisis, that lasted approximately 270,000 years and saw the entire basin virtually isolated from the world ocean. The basin experienced severe desiccation and the precipitation of vast deposits of evaporites (such as salt and gypsum) up to several kilometres in thickness. The Atlantic Ocean subsequently refilled the basin from the west at the beginning of the Zanclean Age. Geologic evidence suggests that water rushing through a channel cut near Gibraltar filled some 90 percent of the Mediterranean Sea within two years. Some scientists contend that sea levels may have risen 10 metres (about 33 feet) per day within the basin during the period of peak flow. The Mediterranean basin has undergone significant geologic evolution during the most recent five million years. About one million years ago, this part of the Tethys was transformed into the Mediterranean Sea by the elevation of the Gibraltar sill. Consequently, the Mediterranean basin became isolated from deep oceanic bottom waters, and the present-day pattern of circulation developed.

In the Northern Hemisphere, the fragmentation of the northern supercontinent of Laurasia, which occurred as the result of the separation of Eurasia from North

MAJOR NEOGENE PALEOGEOGRAPHIC EVENTS*		
AGE	TIME**	PALEOGEOGRAPHIC EVENTS
Pleistocene	c. 1 mya	Uplift of Gibraltar sill and development of present-day Mediterranean circulation patterns (surface water inflow, deep water outflow).
Middle Pliocene	3 mya	Uplift of the Isthmus of Panama, joining North and South America.
Early Pliocene	c. 5 mya	Opening of the Strait of Gibraltar.
Late Miocene	c. 5.5 mya	Closure of the Betic and Riffian (Moroccan) corridor, isolation of western Tethyan Sea from global ocean circulation, and evaporation of the basin.
Middle Miocene	c. 13 mya	Final severance of the Tethys and Paratethys (epeiric continental seaway in southwestern Eurasia).
Early Miocene	c. 18 mya	Junction of Africa and Eurasia.

*Listed are those paleogeographic events that affected global ocean circulation and certain climatic and faunal and floral migration patterns.
**Mya = millions of years ago.

America and Greenland, was accomplished with the opening of the Norwegian-Greenland Sea about 55 million years ago during the Eocene Epoch. Prior to this time, the Greenland-Scotland Ridge formed the Thulean Land Bridge, a continental connection that allowed the exchange of terrestrial mammals between western Eurasia and eastern North America. The subsidence of this ridge during the early Eocene allowed the exchange of surface water between the Arctic and Atlantic oceans. The termination of the Thulean land connection led to the development of separate patterns of evolution among terrestrial vertebrates in Europe and North America.

On the Eurasian continent itself, the Ural Trough, a marine seaway that linked the Tethys with the Arctic region but also constituted a barrier to the east-west migration of terrestrial faunas, was terminated by regional uplift at the end of the Eocene. The resulting immigration of Eurasian land animals into western Europe, and the consequent changes that occurred in terrestrial vertebrates, is known among vertebrate paleontologists as the Grande Coupure (French: "Big Break").

The Bering Land Bridge, which united Siberia and Alaska, served as a second connection between Eurasia and North America. This link seems to have been breached by the Arctic and Pacific oceans between five and seven million years ago, allowing the transit of cold water currents and marine faunas between the Pacific and Atlantic oceans. The Atlantic and Pacific were also linked by the Central American seaway in the area of present-day Costa Rica and Panama. This seaway, extant since the first half of the Cretaceous Period, prevented the interchange of terrestrial fauna between North and South America. For a brief interlude during the Paleocene, however, a land connection may have existed between North and South

America across the volcanic archipelago of the Greater Antillean arc. The seaway was closed by the elevation of the Central American isthmus between 5.5 and 3 million years ago. This event had two significant geologic results. First, the emergence of the isthmus permitted a major migration in land mammal faunas between North and South America (the so-called Great American Interchange), which allowed ground sloths and other South American immigrants to move into North America as far as California, the Great Plains, and Florida. In addition, some North American mammals (such as cats, horses, elephants, and camels) migrated as far south as Patagonia. Second, the emergence of the isthmus deflected the westward-flowing North Equatorial Current toward the north and enhanced the northward-flowing Gulf Stream. This newly invigorated current carried warm, salty waters into high northern latitudes, which contributed to increased rates of evaporation over the oceans and greater precipitation over the region of eastern Canada and Greenland. This pattern eventually led to the formation and development of the polar ice cap in the Northern Hemisphere between 3.5 and 2.5 million years ago. Deflection of the Equatorial Current also changed circulation patterns throughout the Caribbean, Gulf of Mexico, and western North Atlantic, which may have altered patterns of oceanic productivity in the region, resulting in significant evolutionary changes (extinctions and originations) in marine faunas.

PALEOCLIMATE

Climatic history is intimately linked to the dynamic evolution of ocean-continent geometry and the associated changes in oceanic circulation. It is also closely connected to the cycling of carbon through the chemical reservoirs of living and dead organic matter, oceans and atmosphere, and the sediments of Earth's crust. During the Tertiary Period, the continued fragmentation of the world ocean caused by changing positions of the main continental masses (principally a poleward shift in the Northern Hemisphere) led to less efficient latitudinal (east-west) exchange of thermal energy. Paleobiogeographic and oxygen isotope studies support this view by providing evidence of a long-term global temperature decline, the formation and development of a thermally stratified ocean, with much warmer water at the surface and much cooler water at depth, and enhanced climatic differentiation during the Cenozoic. This long-term global temperature decline followed the "climatic optimum" at the Paleocene-Eocene boundary, called the Paleocene-Eocene Thermal Maximum (PETM), that occurred about 55.8 million years ago, which is also reflected in the oxygen isotope records. In general terms, Mesozoic oceanic circulation was latitudinal, and the longitudinal (meridional; north-south) transport of heat energy during that time was relatively inefficient. In contrast, although Cenozoic circulation has been predominantly longitudinal, longitudinal heat transport became increasingly less efficient during the Neogene as global temperatures decreased.

During the Paleocene, warm equable climates extended from one polar region to the other. The mean temperature difference between each pole and the Equator was about 5°C (9°F), whereas today it is about 25°C (45°F). Even deep ocean waters were relatively warm during the Tertiary. The Paleocene-Eocene boundary was marked by a geologically brief episode (less than 100,000 years) of global warming involving elevated temperatures in high-latitude ocean waters, a decline in oceanic productivity, and a marked reduction in global wind intensity. There is considerable evidence that this event was caused

THE PALEOCENE-EOCENE THERMAL MAXIMUM (PETM)

The Paleocene-Eocene Thermal Maximum (PETM), which is also known as the Initial Eocene Thermal Maximum (IETM), was a short interval of maximum temperature lasting approximately 100,000 years during the late Paleocene and early Eocene epochs (roughly 55 million years ago). The interval was characterized by the highest global temperatures of the Cenozoic Era (65 million years ago to the present).

Although the underlying causes are unclear, some authorities associate the PETM with the sudden release of methane hydrates from ocean sediments triggered by a massive volcanic eruption. The onset of the PETM was rapid, occurring within a few thousand years, and the ecological consequences were large, with widespread extinctions in both marine and terrestrial ecosystems. Sea surface and continental air temperatures increased by more than 5°C (9°F) during the transition into the PETM. Sea surface temperatures in the high-latitude Arctic may have been as warm as 23°C (73°F), comparable to modern subtropical and warm-temperate seas.

Following the PETM, global temperatures declined to pre-PETM levels, however, they gradually increased to near-PETM levels over the next few million years during a period known as the Eocene Optimum. This temperature maximum was followed by a steady decline in global temperatures toward the boundary between the Eocene and Oligocene epochs, which occurred about 34 million years ago. Evidence of this global temperature decline is well represented in marine sediments and in paleontological records from the continents, where vegetation zones moved toward the Equator.

by the dissolution of methane hydrates on the ocean floor, which led to an abruptly increased greenhouse effect in the atmosphere.

Fossil remains of tropical faunas such as mollusks and sharks in places such as Alaska and the island of Spitsbergen in the Norwegian Arctic and of reptiles and mammals on Ellesmere Island in the Canadian Arctic Archipelago attest to the subtropical conditions that existed at high latitudes during the early Eocene. Global cooling began during the middle and late Eocene and accelerated rapidly across the Eocene-Oligocene boundary, thereby initiating the process of continental-scale glaciation in Antarctica. In addition, the cooler oceans of the early Oligocene may have been more productive than oceans of the late Eocene.

Ice sheets developed at sea level on West Antarctica during the early Oligocene and covered most of the continent by the middle of the Miocene Epoch about 13 million years ago. The virtually complete glaciation of Antarctica in the late Miocene about 5.5 million years ago has been associated with the isolation of the Mediterranean basin from the world ocean during the Messinian salinity crisis. The sequestration of significant volumes of salt in the

Perito Moreno Glacier, Los Glaciares National Park, Argentina. Jeremy Woodhouse—Digital Vision/Getty Images

Mediterranean basin changed the density of Atlantic deep water and reduced heat transfer from low latitudes to high latitudes. Mountain glaciers appeared in the Gulf of Alaska by the mid-Miocene and were followed by glaciers in Patagonian Argentina during the early Pliocene. The large ice sheets that eventually covered most of northern Europe, Greenland, and North America first formed about 3.5 million years ago, but a major expansion occurred 2.5 million years ago. Many authorities suggest that Earth may have passed over a thermal threshold that initiated an interval of clustered glacial periods, or ice ages, at this time, a mode in which Earth remains locked today. The repeated waxing and waning of the Northern Hemispheric glaciers over the past 2.5 million years has resulted in significant and repeated expansions of the high-latitude belts of westerly winds toward the Equator, changes in ocean circulation pattern, and, during cold phases, the southward displacement of cool, dry climatic belts to southern Europe, the Americas, and North Africa.

TERTIARY LIFE

The end of the Mesozoic Era marked a major transition in Earth's biological history. A major extinction event took place that resulted in the loss of nearly 80 percent of marine and terrestrial animal species. Plant life also suffered, but to a much lesser extent. Most authorities believe that the cause of this major extinction event was one or more impacts by a comet or a meteorite near Chicxulub, Mex., on the Yucatán Peninsula, but some authorities point to the massive volcanic eruptions of the Deccan Traps in India as an additional potential causal factor. In any case, the beginning of the Tertiary Period, which coincided with the onset of the Cenozoic Era, was marked by a reduction in biological diversity both on land and in the

THE METHANE BURP HYPOTHESIS

In oceanography and climatology, the methane burp hypothesis, also called the gas hydrate dissociation hypothesis, is an explanation of the sudden onset of the Paleocene-Eocene Thermal Maximum (PETM). According to the hypothesis, the PETM was triggered when large deposits of methane hydrates in ocean sediments were warmed to the point at which methane was released through the ocean and into the atmosphere in large quantities. The methane then oxidized, forming carbon dioxide. The increase in the concentration of carbon dioxide led to atmospheric warming, perhaps similar to the global warming observed in the 21st century. Large-scale submarine landslides discovered off the coast of Florida have significantly supported the hypothesis, but such landslides would have had to occur in many additional locations to provide enough methane to cause the PETM.

oceans. This reduction was followed by a gradual recovery and an adaptive radiation, or rapid diversification, into new life-forms within a few hundred thousand to several million years. Present-day ecosystems are for the most part populated by animals, plants, and single-celled organisms that survived and redeployed after the great extinction event at the end of the Mesozoic. Groups of organisms such as insects, flowering plants, and marine snails showed particularly rapid diversification after the Mesozoic, and life at the end of the Tertiary was more diverse than ever.

FLOWERING PLANTS AND GRASSES

The Cretaceous-Tertiary transition was not marked by significant changes in terrestrial floras. Throughout the

The impact of a near-Earth object 65 million years ago in what is today the Caribbean region, as depicted in an artist's conception. Many scientists believe that the collision of a large asteroid or comet nucleus with Earth triggered the mass extinction of the dinosaurs and many other species near the end of the Cretaceous Period. NASA; illustration by Don Davis

Cenozoic, angiosperms (flowering plants) continued the remarkable radiation begun roughly 100 million years ago during the middle of the Cretaceous Period and quickly came to dominate most terrestrial habitats (today accounting for approximately 80 percent of all known plant species). Of particular interest among flowering plants are the grasses, which appeared by the late Paleocene Epoch. Simple grasslands, which bore grass but lacked the complex structural organization of sod, appeared in the Eocene, whereas short grasslands with sod appeared in the first half of the Miocene. The Miocene also saw the dramatic expansion of grazing mammals on several continents. Truly modern grasslands appeared in the late Miocene, five to eight million years ago, during a period of cooling and drying that may have been connected to the Messinian salinity crisis in the Mediterranean. The proportion of grasses using the C_4 photosynthetic pathway also increased at this time, consistent with a decrease in atmospheric carbon dioxide at this time.

BIRDS

The number of bird species increased significantly in the Tertiary and throughout the Cenozoic, with separate groups diversifying at different times and places. Among the more notable events in the evolution of birds was the emergence of large flightless birds (*Diatryma* and related forms) during the Paleocene and Eocene epochs. These birds reached heights of more than 2 metres (6.5 feet) and have generally been interpreted as running carnivores, inhabiting the ecological niche left vacant by the extinction of a group of dinosaurs called the theropods at the end of the

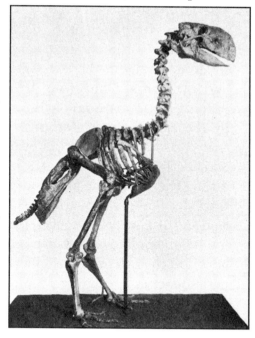

Cast reconstruction of Diatryma *skeleton.* Courtesy of the American Museum of Natural History, New York

Cretaceous. A similar interpretation has been given to the even larger flightless birds of the Oligocene of South America (such as *Phorusrhacos* and related forms), which evolved when South America was an island continent, isolated from advanced mammalian carnivores.

The passerines are the most diverse group of modern birds. They have a poor fossil record and may have emerged as early as the Early Cretaceous or as late as the Oligocene. Passerines began an explosive period of diversification during the Miocene.

THE RISE OF MAMMALS

The most spectacular event in Cenozoic terrestrial environments has been the diversification and rise to dominance of the mammals. From only a few groups of small mammals in the late Cretaceous that lived in the undergrowth and hid from the dinosaurs, more than 20 orders of mammals rapidly evolved and were established by the early Eocene. Although there is some evidence that this adaptive radiation event began well before the end of the Cretaceous, rates of speciation accelerated during the Paleocene and Eocene epochs. At the end of the Paleocene, a major episode of faunal turnover (extinction and origination) largely replaced many archaic groups (multituberculates, plesiadapids, and "condylarth" ungulates) with essentially modern groups such as the perissodactyls (including primitive horses, rhinoceroses, and tapirs), artiodactyls (such as camels and deer), rodents, rabbits, bats, proboscideans, and primates.

In the Eocene these groups dispersed widely, migrating via a northern route, probably from Eurasia to North America. In the late Eocene an episode of global cooling triggered changes in the vegetation that converted areas of thick rainforest to more open forest and grasslands,

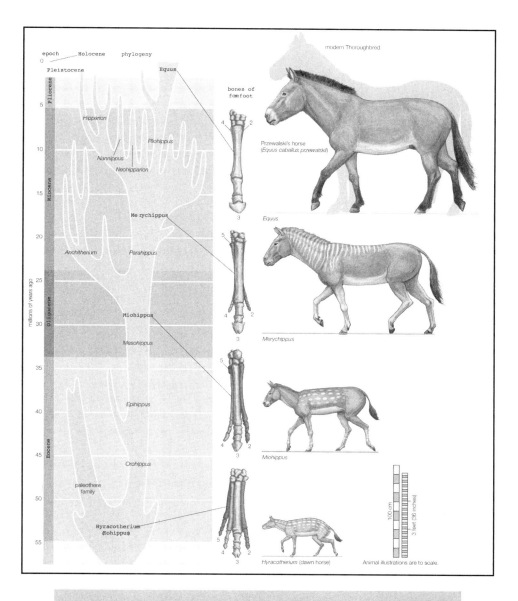

Evolution of the horse over the past 55 million years. The present-day Przewalski's horse is believed to be the only remaining example of a wild horse (i.e., the last remaining modern horse to have evolved by natural selection). Numbered bones in the forefoot illustrations trace the gradual transition from a four-toed to a one-toed animal. Encyclopædia Britannica, Inc.

thereby causing another interval of evolutionary turnover that included the disappearance of the last of the primitive herbivores, such as the brontotheres. From the Oligocene Epoch onward, land mammal communities were dominated by representatives of the mammalian groups living today, such as horses, rhinoceroses, antelopes, deer, camels, elephants, felines, and canines.

These groups evolved significantly during the Miocene as the changes to climate and vegetation produced more open grassy habitat. Starting with primitive forms that had low-crowned teeth for browsing leafy vegetation, many herbivorous mammals evolved specialized teeth for grazing gritty grasses and long limbs for running and escaping from increasingly efficient predators. By the late Miocene, grassland communities analogous to those present in the modern savannas of East Africa were established on most continents. Evolution within many groups of terrestrial mammals since the late Miocene has been strongly affected by the dramatic climate fluctuations of the late Cenozoic.

MAMMALIAN MIGRATION FROM EURASIA TO NORTH AMERICA

The rapid evolutionary diversification or radiation of mammals in the early Tertiary was probably mostly a response to the removal of reptilian competitors by the mass extinction event occurring at the end of the Cretaceous Period. Later events in mammalian evolution, however, may have occurred in response to changes in geology, geography, and climatic conditions. In the middle of the Eocene Epoch, for example, the direct migration of land mammals between North America and Europe was interrupted by the severance of the Thulean Land Bridge, a connection that had existed prior to this time. Although Europe became cut off from North America, Asia (especially Siberia) remained in contact with Alaska during the late Eocene, and repeated migrations occurred throughout the Oligocene and Miocene epochs.

During the early Miocene, a wave of mammalian immigration from Eurasia brought bear-dogs (early ancestors of modern canines of the genus *Amphicyon*), European rhinoceroses, weasels, and a variety of deerlike mammals to North America. Also during this time, mastodons escaped from their isolation in Africa and reached North America by the middle of the Miocene. Horses and rodents evolved in the early Eocene, and anthropoid primates emerged during the middle Eocene. Immigration of African mammalian faunas, including proboscideans (mammoths, mastodons, and other relatives of modern elephants), into Europe occurred about 18 million years ago (early Miocene). Climatic cooling and drying during the Miocene led to several episodes where grassland ecosystems expanded and concomitant evolutionary diversifications of grazing mammals occurred.

MAMMALIAN MIGRATION BETWEEN NORTH AND SOUTH AMERICA

During the late Pliocene, the land bridge formed by the Central American isthmus allowed opossums, porcupines, armadillos, and ground sloths to migrate from South America and live in the southern United States. A much larger wave of typically Northern Hemispheric animals, however, moved south and may have contributed to the extinction of most of the mammals endemic to South America. These North American invaders included dogs and wolves, raccoons, cats, horses, tapirs, llamas, peccaries, and mastodons.

PRIMATES

Amid the rapid diversification of mammals in the early Tertiary, primates evolved from animals similar to modern squirrels and tree shrews. Compared with other terrestrial mammals, primates possessed the largest brains relative to their body weight. This feature—along with limb extremities composed of flat nails rather than hooves or claws, specialized nerve endings called Meissner's corpuscles that increased the tactile sensitivity in their hands and feet, and rounded molars and premolar cusps—allowed primates to adapt to and exploit arboreal environments and newly emergent grasslands. Although the first signs of primate dentition were present as early as the Paleocene Epoch, the first fully recognizable primate forms did not emerge until the Eocene. Members of the Tarsiidae (including modern tarsiers and their ancestors) appeared in western Europe and North Africa, the Adapidae (such as lemurs, lorises, and their ancestors) arose in North America and Europe, and the Omomyidae (including the possible ancestors of monkeys and apes) emerged in North America, Europe, Egypt, and Asia during the Eocene Epoch. In addition, fossil evidence indicates that the earliest monkeylike primates (Simiiformes) arose in China about 45 million years ago.

The separation of the more primitive primates (lemurs, lorises, tarsiers, and their ancestors) from the more advanced forms (monkeys, apes, and humans) is thought to have occurred during the Oligocene Epoch. The skull of *Rooneyia*, an omomyid fossil discovered in Texas and dated to the Oligocene, possesses a mixture of primitive and advanced features and is thus considered to be a transitional primate form. Some primate groups abandoned the locomotor patterns of vertical clinging and leaping for quadrupedalism (walking on four limbs) during the

Oligocene. Other developments include the emergence of the catarrhines (Old World monkeys, apes, and humans) in Africa and the platyrrhines (New World monkeys) in South America. The catarrhines are the only group to possess truly opposable thumbs. (Some lower primates possess nominally opposable thumbs but lack the precision grip of catarrhines.)

By the Miocene, because of dramatic changes in Earth's geomorphology and climate and the emergence of vast grasslands, a new type of primate—the ground inhabitant—came into being. The benefit of a generalized body form and a larger brain assisted many primates in their transition to terrestrial lifestyles. During this time, *Sivapithecus*—a form considered to be the direct ancestor of orangutans—appeared in Eurasia, and *Dryopithecus*—the direct ancestor of gorillas, chimpanzees, and humans—appeared in parts of Africa and Eurasia. In addition, *Morotopithecus bishopi*, a species possessing the earliest traces of the modern hominoid skeletal features, appeared some 20 million years ago near Lake Victoria in Africa.

The late Miocene-Pliocene primate fossil record is surprisingly sparse. No fossils traceable to the lineages of modern apes are known, and only meagre information exists for monkey families. Nevertheless, this interval is perhaps best known for the rise of the human lineage in central and eastern Africa, as evidenced by *Sahelanthropus tchadensis* from Chad (7 million years ago), *Orrorin tugenensis* from Kenya (6.1–5.8 million years ago), and *Ardipithecus ramidus* (4.4 million years ago). *Ardipithecus* has an expanded tarsal region on each foot, and its foramen (the hole in the skull through which the spinal cord enters) is located centrally under the skull instead of at the rear of it. In addition, the design of the pelvis of *Ardipithecus* is similar to that of more advanced hominins. These features are indicative of bipedalism, one of the characteristics that separate the human lineage from those of apes and chimpanzees. Other bipedal primates from the Pliocene include *Kenyanthropus platyops* and various species of *Australopithecus*. The precise evolutionary relationships among these forms remain controversial, but it is clear that they lie close to the evolutionary branching event that separates humans from apes.

LIFE IN THE OCEANS

The Tertiary Period was also a time of opportunity for marine species. As life in the oceans recovered from the K–T extinction (a global extinction event responsible for eliminating approximately 80% of all species of animals), marine invertebrates, foraminiferans, and large marine mammals underwent rapid radiations. Some of the more notable forms included mollusks and corals, nummulites, and whales.

MARINE EXTINCTIONS AND RECOVERY

In the seas, several major Tertiary biotic events stand out. The major extinction event at the boundary between the Mesozoic and Cenozoic eras, 65.5 million years ago, affected not only the dinosaurs of the terrestrial environments but also large marine reptiles, marine invertebrate faunas (rudists, belemnites, ammonites, bivalves), planktonic protozoans (foraminiferans), and phytoplankton. The recovery of biological diversity after this event took hundreds of thousands to millions of years, depending on the group. At the boundary between the Paleocene and the Eocene, between 30 and 50 percent of all species of deep-sea benthic foraminiferans became extinct in a sudden event associated with the warming of the deep oceans. The present-day fauna of the deep, cold oceans (the so-called psychrosphere) evolved in the latest part of the Eocene about 35 million years ago. This was concomitant with a significant cooling of oceanic deep waters of some 3–5°C (5.4–9°F). The transition between the Eocene and Oligocene was also marked by several extinction events among marine faunas. The closure of the Tethys seaway in the late Early Miocene about 15 million years ago resulted in the disappearance of many of the larger tropical foraminiferans called nummulitids (large lens-shaped foraminiferans) whose habitat ranged from Indonesia to Spain and as far north as Paris and London. Although the descendants of nummulitids can be found today in the Indo-Pacific region, they show much less diversity.

The marine faunas of the eastern Pacific and western Atlantic region were similar throughout the Tertiary until about 3–5.5 million years ago. The elevation of the Central American isthmus at that time created a land barrier between the two regions that during the Tertiary resulted in the isolation of one fauna from another and differentiation (that is, "provincialization") between the groups. In addition, the presence of the isthmus may have led to environmental changes in the western Atlantic that caused high rates of extinction in old species and the origination of new ones.

THE RADIATION OF INVERTEBRATES

In the oceans, patterns of evolution that had begun during the Cretaceous Period continued and in some cases accelerated during the Tertiary. These include the evolutionary radiation of crabs, bony fish, snails, and clams. An increase in predation may have been an important driving force of evolution in the sea during this time. Many groups of clams and snails, for example, show increased adaptations for resisting predators during the Tertiary. Episodes of rapid diversification also occurred in many groups of clams and snails during the Eocene Epoch and at the Miocene-Pliocene boundary. Following the extinction of the reef-building rudists (large bivalve mollusks) at the end of the Cretaceous, reef-building corals had recovered by the Eocene, and their low-latitude continuous stratigraphic record is taken as an indicator of the persistence of the tropical realm.

LARGE MARINE ANIMALS

Cetaceans (whales and their relatives) first appeared in the early Eocene, about 51 million years ago, and are thought to have evolved from early artiodactyls (a group of hoofed mammals possessing an even number of toes). Whale evolution accelerated during the Oligocene and Miocene, and this is probably associated with an increase in oceanic productivity. Other new marine forms that emerged in late Paleogene seas were the penguins, a group of swimming birds, and the pinnipeds (a group of mammals that includes seals, sea lions, and walruses). The largest marine carnivore of the period was the shark (*Carcharocles megalodon*), which lived from the middle Miocene to the late Pliocene and reached lengths of at least 16 metres (about 50 feet).

FORAMINIFERANS

Foraminiferans, especially those belonging to superfamily Globigerinacea, also evolved rapidly and dispersed widely during the Tertiary Period. Consequently, they have proved to be extremely useful as indicators in efforts to correlate oceanic sediments and uplifted marine strata at global and regional scales. Differential rates of evolution within separate groups of foraminiferans increase the utility of some forms in delineating stratigraphic zones, a step in the process of correlating rocks of similar age. For example, conical species of *Morozovella* and *Globorotalia* are often used to correlate rock strata across vast geographies because they have wide stratigraphic ranges that vary from one to five million years.

The nummulitids were a group of large lens-shaped foraminiferans that inhabited the bottoms of shallow-water tropical marine realms. They had complex labyrinthine interiors and internal structural supports to strengthen their adaptation to life in high-energy environments. Nummulitids also received nourishment from single-celled symbiotic algae (tiny photosynthetic dinoflagellates) they housed within their bodies. Nummulitids of the genus *Nummulites* grew to substantial size (up to 150 mm [6 inches] in diameter), and they occurred in massive numbers during a major transgression taking place during the middle of the Eocene Epoch. This transgression produced high sea levels and formed extensive limestone deposits in Egypt, which produced the blocks from which the pyramids were built. *Nummulites* lived throughout the Eurasian-Tethyan faunal province from the later part of the Paleocene Epoch to the early Oligocene, but it did not reach the Western Hemisphere. Following the extinction of *Nummulites*, other larger foraminiferans, the miogypsinids and lepidocyclinids, flourished.

TERTIARY ROCKS

Although the descriptor *Tertiary rocks* is slowly being replaced by the terms *Paleogene rocks* and *Neogene rocks*, it was a useful category for many years. Initially developed by Italian geologist Giovanni Arduino, the descriptor was used to describe sedimentary sequences occurring at lower elevations that were made up of neither gravels and pebbles nor shales and limestones. More recently, it has been used to describe the sedimentary deposits of several

European and North American basins, the volcanism associated with the creation of Iceland and the Hawaiian island chain, and the mountain-building events that created the Himalayas. In addition, the discipline of geology owes many of its advances, such as the development of modern dating techniques and fossil correlation, to the study of Tertiary rocks in particular.

THE MAJOR SUBDIVISIONS OF THE TERTIARY SYSTEM

Classically, the Cenozoic Era was divided into the Tertiary and Quaternary periods, separated at the boundary between the Pliocene and Pleistocene epochs (formerly set at 1.8 million years ago). By the late 20th century, however, many authorities considered the terms Tertiary and Quaternary to be obsolete. In 2005 the ICS decided to recommend keeping the Tertiary and Quaternary periods as units in the geologic time scale, but only as sub-eras within the Cenozoic Era. By 2009 the larger intervals (periods and epochs) of the Cenozoic had been formalized by the ICS and the International Union of Geological Sciences (IUGS). The ICS redivided the Cenozoic Era into the Paleogene Period (65.5 to 23 million years ago), the Neogene Period (23 million to 2.6 million years ago), and the Quaternary Period (2.6 million years ago to the present). Under this paradigm, the Paleogene and Neogene span the interval formerly occupied by the Tertiary. The Paleogene Period, the oldest of the three divisions, commences at the onset of the Cenozoic Era and includes the Paleocene Epoch (65.5 million to 55.8 million years ago), the Eocene Epoch (55.8 million to 33.9 million years ago), and the Oligocene Epoch (33.9 million to 23 million years ago). The Neogene spans the interval between the beginning of the Miocene Epoch (23 million to 5.3 million years ago) and the end of the Pliocene Epoch (5.3 million to 2.6 million years ago). The Quaternary Period begins at the base of the Pleistocene Epoch (2.6 million to 11,700 years ago) and continues through the Holocene Epoch (11,700 years ago to the present).

Precise stratigraphic positions for the boundaries of the various traditional Tertiary series were not specified by early workers in the 19th century. It is only in more recent times that the international geologic community has formulated a philosophical framework for stratigraphy. By specifying the lower limits of rock units deposited during successive increments of geologic time at designated points in the rock record (called stratotypes), geologists have established a series of calibration points, called a Global Stratotype Section and Point (GSSP), at which time and rock coincide. These boundary stratotypes are the linchpins of global chronostratigraphic units—essentially, the points of reference that mark time within the rock—and serve as the point of departure for global correlation.

Several boundary stratotypes have been identified within Tertiary rocks. The Cretaceous–Tertiary, or K–T, boundary has been stratotypified in Tunisia in North Africa. (Increasingly, this boundary is known as the Cretaceous–Paleogene, or K–P, boundary.) Its estimated age is 65.5 million years. The Paleocene-Eocene boundary has an estimated age of 55.8 million years, and its GSSP is located near Luxor, Egypt. In the early 1990s the Eocene–Oligocene boundary was stratotypically established in southern Italy, with a currently estimated age of approximately 33.9 million years. The Oligocene-Miocene boundary, which also corresponds to the boundary between the Paleogene and Neogene systems, has been stratotyped in Carrosio, Italy. It is calculated at roughly 23 million years old. Although the GSSP associated with the

Miocene-Pliocene boundary is located in Sicily and has been dated to about 5.3 million years ago, the location of this boundary may be repositioned in the future. The boundary between the Pliocene and the Pleistocene, separating the Neogene and Quaternary systems, has been stratotyped in Sicily near the town of Gela and dated to approximately 2.6 million years ago.

THE OCCURRENCE AND DISTRIBUTION OF TERTIARY DEPOSITS

With the exception of the vast Tethys seaway, the basins of western Europe, and the extensive Mississippi Embayment of the Gulf Coast region in the United States, Tertiary marine deposits are located predominantly along continental margins and occur on all continents. Miocene deposits are found as far north as Alaska, Eocene deposits in eastern Canada, and Paleocene deposits in Greenland. Deposits of Paleogene age occur on Seymour Island near the Antarctic Peninsula, and Neogene deposits containing marine diatoms (silica-bearing marine phytoplankton) have recently been identified intercalated between glacial tills on Antarctica.

Global sea levels have fallen gradually by about 300 metres (about 1,000 feet) over the past 100 million years, but superimposed on that trend is a higher order series of globally fluctuating increases and decreases (that is, transgressions and regressions) in sea level. These fluctuations vary with a periodicity of several million years. Where they have occurred along passive (that is, tectonically stable) continental margins, they have left a record of marginal marine, brackish accumulations that overlap with continental sedimentary deposits in Europe, North Africa, the Middle East, southern Australia, and the Gulf and Atlantic coastal plains of North America. In most regions, Paleogene seas extended farther inland than did those of the Neogene. In fact, the most extensive transgression of the Tertiary is that of the Lutetian Age (Middle Eocene), about 49–40 million years ago. During that interval, the Tethys Sea expanded onto the continental margins of Africa and Eurasia and left extensive deposits of nummulitic rocks, which are made up of shallow water carbonates. Sediments of Tertiary age are widely developed on the deep ocean floor and on elevated seamounts as well. In the shallower parts of the ocean (above depths of 4.5 km [about 3 miles]), sediments are calcareous (made of calcium carbonate), siliceous (derived from silica), or both, depending on local productivity. Below 4.5 km the sediments are principally siliceous or inorganic, as in the case of red clay, as a result of dissolution of calcium carbonate.

Nonmarine Tertiary sedimentary and volcanic deposits are widespread in North America, particularly in the intermontane basins west of the Mississippi River. During the Neogene, volcanism and terrigenous deposition extended almost to the Pacific coast. In South America, thick nonmarine clastic sequences (conglomerates, sandstones, and shales) occur in the mobile tectonic belt of the Andes Mountains and along their eastern front in sequences that extend eastward for a considerable distance into the Amazon basin. Tertiary marine deposits occur along the eastern margins of Brazil and Argentina, and they were already known to English naturalist Charles Darwin during his exploration of South America from 1832 to 1834.

VOLCANISM AND OROGENESIS

Volcanism has continued throughout the Cenozoic on land and at the major oceanic ridges, such as the Mid-Atlantic Ridge and the East Pacific Rise, where new seafloor is continuously generated and carried away later-ally by seafloor spreading. Formed in the middle Miocene, Iceland is one of the few places where the processes that occur at the Mid-Atlantic Ridge can be observed today.

Two of the most extensive volcanic outpourings recorded in the geologic record occurred during the Tertiary. About 67–66 million years ago, near the Cretaceous–Tertiary boundary, massive outpourings of basaltic lava formed the Deccan Traps of India. About 55 million years ago, near the Paleocene–Eocene boundary, massive explosive volcanism took place in northwestern Scotland, northern Ireland, the Faeroe Islands, East Greenland, and along the rifted continental margins on both sides of the North Atlantic Ocean. Volcanic activity in the North Atlantic was associated with the rifting and separation of Eurasia from North America, which occurred on a line between Scandinavia and Greenland and left a stratigraphic record in the marine sedimentary basin of England and in ash deposits as far south as the Bay of Biscay. In both the Deccan and North Atlantic, comparable volumes of extensive basalts in the amount of 10,000,000 cubic km (about 2,400,000 cubic miles) were erupted.

The well-known volcanics of the Massif Central of south-central France, which figured so prominently in early (18th-century) investigations into the nature of igne-ous rocks, are of Oligocene age, as are those located in central Germany. The East African Rift System preserves a record of mid-to-late Tertiary rifting and the separation event that eventually led to the formation of a marine sea-way linking the Indian Ocean with the Mediterranean.

The circum-Pacific "Ring of Fire," an active tectonic belt that extends from the Philippines through Japan and around the west coast of North and South America, was subject to seismic activity and andesitic volcanism throughout much of the Tertiary. The extensive Columbia Plateau basalts were extruded over Washington and Oregon during the Miocene, and many volcanoes of Alaska, Oregon, southern Idaho, and northeastern California date to the Late Tertiary. Active volcanism occurred in the newly uplifted Rocky Mountains during the early part of the Tertiary, whereas in the southern Rocky Mountains and Mexico volcanic activity was more common in the mid- and late Tertiary. The linear volcanic trends, such as the Hawaiian, Emperor, and Line island chains in the central and northwestern Pacific, are trails resulting from the movement of the Pacific Plate over volcanic hot spots (that is, magma-generating centres) that are probably fixed deep in Earth's mantle. The major hot spot island groups such as the Hawaiian (which has been active over the past 30 million years), Galápagos, and Society (which were active during the Miocene) islands are volcanoes that rose from the seafloor. Central America, the Caribbean region, and northern South America were the sites of active volcanism throughout the Cenozoic.

In contrast to the passive-margin sedimentation on the Atlantic and Gulf coastal plains, the Cordilleran (or Laramide) orogeny in the Late Cretaceous, Paleocene, and Eocene produced a series of upfolded and upthrusted mountains and deep intermontane basins in the area of the Rocky Mountains. Deeply downwarped basins accumulated as much as 2,400 metres (about 8,000 feet) of Paleocene and Eocene sediment in the Green River Basin of southwestern Wyoming and 4,300 metres (about 14,000 feet) of sediment in the Uinta Basin of northeastern Utah. Other basins ranging from Montana to New Mexico accumulated similar but thinner packages of non-marine fluvial and lacustrine sediments rich in fossil mammals and fish. In the Oligocene and Miocene, the influences of the cordilleras, or mountain chains, on what is now the western United States had ceased, and the basins were gradually filled to the top by sediments and abundant volcanic ash deposits from eruptions in present-day Colorado, Nevada, and Utah. These basins were exhumed during the former Pliocene–Pleistocene boundary (about 1.8 million years ago) with renewed uplift of the long-buried Rocky Mountains, along with uplift of the Colorado Plateau, producing steep stream gradients that resulted in the cutting of the Grand Canyon to a depth of more than 1,800 metres (about 6,000 feet).

Volcanism along the Cascade mountain chain has been active since the late Eocene, as evidenced by the major eruption of Mount St. Helens in 1980 and subsequent minor eruptions. This volcanism was gradually shut off in California as the movement of plate boundaries changed from one of subduction to a sliding and transform motion. With the development of the San Andreas Fault system, the western half of California started sliding northward. The Cascade–Sierra Nevada mountain chain began to swing clockwise, causing the extension of the Basin and Range Province in Nevada, Arizona, and western Utah. This crustal extension broke the Basin and Range into a series of north-south-trending fault-block mountains and downdropped basins, which filled with thousands of metres of upper Cenozoic sediment. These fault zones (particularly the Wasatch Fault in central Utah and the San Andreas zone in California) remain active today and are the source of most of the damaging earthquakes in North America. The Andean mountains were uplifted during the Neogene as a result of subduction of the South Pacific beneath the South American continent.

Complex tectonic activity also occurred in Asia and Europe during the Tertiary. The main Alpine orogeny began during the late Eocene and Oligocene and continued throughout much of the Neogene. Major tectonic activity in the eastern North Atlantic (Bay of Biscay) extended into southern France and culminated in the uplift of the Pyrenees in the late Eocene. On the south side of the Tethys, the coastal Atlas Mountains of North Africa experienced major uplift during this time, but the Betic region of southern Spain and the Atlas region of northern Morocco continued to display mirror-image histories of tectonic activity well into the late Neogene. In the Middle East the suturing of Africa and Asia occurred about 18 million years ago. Elsewhere, India had collided with the Asian continent about 45 million years ago, initiating the Himalayan uplift that was to intensify in the Pliocene and Pleistocene and culminate in the uplift of the great Plateau of Tibet and the Himalayan mountain range. Major orogenic movement also occurred in the Indonesian-Malaysian-Japanese arc system during the Neogene. In New Zealand, which sits astride the Indian-Australian and Pacific plate boundary, the major tectonic uplift (the Kaikoura orogeny) of the Southern Alps began about 10 million years ago.

SEDIMENTARY SEQUENCES

Northwestern Europe contains a number of Tertiary marine basins that essentially rim the North Sea basin, itself the site of active subsidence during the Paleogene and infilling during the Neogene. The marine Hampshire and London basins, the Paris Basin, the Anglo-Belgian Basin, and the North German Basin have become the standard for comparative studies of the Paleogene part of the Cenozoic, whereas the Mediterranean region (Italy) has become the standard for the Neogene. The Tertiary record of the Paris Basin is essentially restricted to the Paleogene strata (namely, those of Paleocene–late Oligocene age), whereas scattered Pliocene-Pleistocene deposits occur in England and Belgium above the Paleogene. The strata are relatively thin, nearly horizontal, and often highly fossiliferous, particularly in the middle Eocene *calcaire grossier* (freshwater limestone) of the Paris Basin, from which a molluscan fauna of more than 500 species has been described. The Paris Basin is a roughly oval-shaped basin centred on Paris, whereas the Hampshire and London basins lie to the southwest and northeast of London, respectively. The London Basin and the Anglo-Belgian Basin were part of a single sedimentary basin across what is now the English Channel during the early part of the Paleogene.

The total Paleogene stratigraphic succession in these basins is less than 300 metres (about 980 feet), and it is made up of clays, marls, sands, carbonates, lignites, and gypsum. These layers reflect alternations of marine, brackish, lacustrine, and terrestrial environments of deposition.

Fossils help geologists establish the ages of layers of rock. In this diagram, sections A and B represent rock layers 200 miles (320 km) apart. Their ages can be established by comparing the fossils in each layer.

The alternating transgressions and regressions of the sea have left a complex sedimentary record punctuated by numerous unconformities (interruptions in the deposition of sedimentary rock) and associated temporal hiatuses, and the correlation of these various units and events has challenged stratigraphers since the early 19th century. The integration of biostratigraphy, paleomagnetic stratigraphy, and tephrochronology (respectively, using fossils, magnetic properties, and ash layers to establish the age and succession of rocks) has resulted in a refined correlation of rock layers in these separate basins.

In North America, by contrast, extensive Tertiary sediments occur on the Atlantic and Gulf coastal plains and extend around the margin of the Gulf of Mexico to the Yucatán Peninsula, a distance of more than 5,000 km (about 3,100 miles). Seaward these deposits can be traced from the Atlantic Coastal Plain to the continental margin and rise and in the Gulf Coastal Plain into the subsurface formations of this oil-bearing province of the Gulf of Mexico. During the Paleocene the Gulf Coast extended northward roughly 2,000 km (about 1,200 miles) in a feature called the Mississippi Embayment, which reached as far as southwestern North Dakota and Montana. There marine deposits known as the Cannonball Formation can be seen as outcrops of sandstone. Although eroded between northwestern South Dakota and southern Illinois, marine outcrops continue southward to the present coastline and continue in the subsurface of the Gulf of Mexico. Tertiary sediments with a thickness in excess of 6,000 metres (about 20,000 feet) are estimated to lie beneath the continental margin along the northern Gulf of Mexico. In the Tampico Embayment of eastern Mexico, thicknesses of more than 3,000 metres (about 10,000 feet) have been estimated for the Paleocene Velasco Formation alone, which developed under conditions of active subsidence and associated rapid deposition. Exposures in the Atlantic Coastal Plain and most of the Gulf Coastal Plain are of Paleogene age, but considerable thicknesses of Neogene sediment occur in offshore wells in front of the Mississippi delta, where thicknesses in excess of 10,000 metres (about 33,000 feet) have been recorded for the Neogene alone. Sediments are dominantly calcareous in the Florida region and become more marly and eventually sandy to the west, reflecting the input of terrigenous matter transported seasonally by the Mississippi River and its precursors. Because of general faunal and floral similarities, it is possible to make relatively precise stratigraphic correlations in the Paleogene between the Gulf and Atlantic coastal plain region and the basins in northwestern Europe.

ESTABLISHING TERTIARY BOUNDARIES

The name Tertiary was introduced by Italian geologist Giovanni Arduino in 1760 as the second-youngest division of Earth's rocks. The oldest rocks were the primitive, or "primary," igneous and metamorphic rocks (composed of schists, granites, and basalts) that formed the core of the high mountains in Europe. Arduino designated rocks composed predominantly of shales and limestones in northern Italy as elements of the fossiliferous "secondary," or Mesozoic, group. He considered younger groups of fossiliferous sedimentary rocks, found chiefly at lower elevations, as "tertiary" rocks and the smaller pebbles and gravel that covered them as "quaternary" rocks. Although originally intended as a descriptive generalization of rock types, many of Arduino's contemporaries and successors gave these categories a temporal connotation and equated them with rocks formed prior to, during, and after the Noachian deluge. In 1810 French mineralogist, geologist,

and naturalist Alexandre Brongniart included all the sedimentary deposits of the Paris Basin in his *terrains tertiares*,
or Tertiary. Soon thereafter all rocks younger than
Mesozoic in western Europe were called Tertiary.

The subdivision of the Tertiary into smaller units was
originally based on fossil faunas of western Europe that
were known to 19th-century natural scientists. These faunas primarily contained mollusks exhibiting varying
degrees of similarity with modern types. At the same time,
the science of stratigraphy was in its infancy, and the primary focus of its earliest practitioners was to use the newly
discovered sequential progression of fossils in layered sedimentary rocks to establish a global sequence of temporally
ordered stages. Scottish geologist Charles Lyell employed
a simple statistical measure based on the relative percentages of living species of mollusks to fossil mollusks found
in different layers of Tertiary rocks. These percentages
had been compiled by Lyell's colleague and friend Gérard-
Paul Deshayes, a French geologist who had amassed a
collection of more than 40,000 mollusks and was prepar-
ing a monograph on the mollusks of the Paris Basin.

In 1833 Lyell divided the Tertiary into four subdivisions (from older to younger): Eocene, Miocene, the "older
Pliocene," and the "newer Pliocene." (The latter was
renamed Pleistocene in 1839.) The Eocene contained
about 3 percent of the living mollusk species, the
Miocene about 20 percent, the older Pliocene more than
33 percent and often over 50 percent, and the newer
Pliocene about 90 percent. Lyell traveled extensively and
had a broad and comprehensive understanding of the
regional geology for his day. He understood, for example,
that rocks of the Tertiary were unevenly distributed over
Europe and that there were no rocks of the younger part
of the period in the Paris Basin. He used the deposits in
the Paris, Hampshire, and London basins as typical for the

Eocene. For the Miocene he used the sediments of the Loire Basin near Touraine, the deposits in the Aquitaine Basin near Bordeaux in southwestern France, and the Bormida River valley and Superga near Turin, Italy. The sub-Apennine formations of northern Italy were used for the older Pliocene, and the marine strata in the Gulf of Noto, on the Island of Ischia (also in Italy), and near Uddevalla (in Sweden) were used for the newer Pliocene.

The limits between Lyell's Tertiary subdivisions were not rigidly specified, and Lyell recognized the approximate and imperfect nature of his scheme. Indeed, in their original form, Lyell's subdivisions would today be termed biostratigraphic units (bodies of rocks characterized by particular fossil assemblages) rather than chronostratigraphic units (bodies of rocks deposited during a specific interval of time).

Subsequent stratigraphic studies in northern Europe showed that deposits were included variously in the upper Eocene or lower Miocene by different geologists of the day. This situation led German geologist H.E. Beyrich, in 1854, to create the term Oligocene for rocks in the North German Basin and Mainz Basin and to insert it between the Eocene and the Miocene in the stratigraphic scheme. As originally proposed, the Oligocene included the Tongrian and Rupelian stages as well as strata that subsequently formed the basis for the Chattian Stage. The Tongrian is no longer used as a standard unit, its place being taken by the Rupelian.

The term Paleocene was proposed by German paleobotanist Wilhelm P. Schimper in 1874 on the basis of fossil floras in the Paris Basin that he considered intermediate between Cretaceous and Eocene forms. Typical strata include the sands of Bracheux, the travertines of Sézanne, and the lignites and sandstones of Soissons. The problem of the Paleocene is that, of all the chronostratigraphic units of the Tertiary, it alone is defined on the basis of non-marine strata, making recognition of its upper limit and general correlation difficult elsewhere. Acceptance of the term Paleocene into the general system of stratigraphic names was irregular, and only in 1939 did the United States Geological Survey, general arbiter of standard stratigraphic nomenclature in North America, formally accept it. The Danian Stage was proposed by the Swiss geologist Pierre Jean Édouard Desor in 1846 for chalk deposits in Denmark. It was assigned to the Cretaceous by virtue of the similarity of its invertebrate megafossils to those of the latest Cretaceous elsewhere. However, since the late 1950s, micropaleontologists have recognized that calcareous marine plankton (foraminiferans and coccolith-bearing nannoplankton) exhibit a major taxonomic change at the boundary between the Maastrichtian (uppermost Cretaceous) Stage and the Danian (lowermost Tertiary) Stage. The Danian is now widely regarded as being the oldest stage of the Cenozoic.

In 1948 the 18th International Geological Congress placed the base of the Pleistocene at the base of the marine strata of the Calabrian Stage of southern Italy, using the initial appearance of northern or cool-water invertebrate faunas in Mediterranean marine strata as the marker. Subsequent studies showed that the type section was ill-chosen and that the base of the Calabrian Stage was equivalent to much younger levels within the Pleistocene. A newly designated stratotype section was chosen at Vrica in Calabria, and for a time the base of the Pleistocene was found comparable to a level dated to nearly 1.8 million years ago. In 2009 the IUGS ratified the decision by the ICS to align the base of the Pleistocene (and thus the top of the Neogene System) with the base of the Gelasian Stage.

THE CORRELATION OF TERTIARY STRATA

The boundaries of the Tertiary were originally only quali-
tatively estimated on the basis of the percentages of living
species of (primarily) mollusks in the succession of marine
strata in the western European basins. The need for more
precise correlations of Mesozoic and Cenozoic marine
strata in Europe led to the concept of stages, which was
introduced in 1842 by French paleontologist Alcide
d'Orbigny. These stages were originally defined as rock
sequences composed of distinctive assemblages of fossils
that were believed to change abruptly as a result of major
transgressions and regressions of the sea. This methodol-
ogy has since been improved and refined, but it forms the
basis for modern biostratigraphic correlation. Although
early attempts at global correlations of strata were made
by direct comparisons with the faunas in the type areas in
Europe, it was soon realized that faunal provincialization
led to spurious correlations. In 1919 an independent set of
percentages for the Indonesian region was proposed,
which was subsequently modified into the so-called East
India Letter Stage classification system based on the
occurrence of taxa of larger foraminiferans.

Since about the mid-1900s, increasing efforts have
been made to apply radioisotopic dating techniques to
the development of a geochronologic scale, particularly
for the Cenozoic Era. The decay of potassium-40 to
argon-40 has proved useful in this respect, and refine-
ments in mass spectroscopy and the development of
laser-fusion dating involving the decay of argon-40 to
argon-39 have resulted in the ability to date volcanic min-
eral samples in amounts as small as single crystals with a
margin of error of less than 1 percent over the span of the
entire Cenozoic Era.

Also, since the mid-1960s, investigators have demonstrated that Earth's magnetic field has undergone numerous reversals in the past. It is known that most rocks pick up and retain the magnetic orientation of the field at the time they are formed through either sedimentary or igneous processes. With the development of techniques for measuring the rock's original orientation of magnetization, a sequence of polarity reversals has been dated for the late Neogene. In addition, a paleomagnetic chronology has been built for the entire Cenozoic. This work is based on the recognition that the magnetic lineations detected in rocks on the ocean floor were formed when basaltic magma had been extruded from the oceanic ridges. Earth's magnetic polarity undergoes a reversal roughly every 500,000 years, and newly formed rocks assume the ambient magnetic polarity of the time. As a result, strips of normal and reversed polarity that reflect these magnetic reversals can be observed in deep-sea cores. The calibration of the composite geomagnetic polarity succession to time and the relation of this chronology to the isotopic time scale, however, have proved to be the greatest source of disagreement over various current versions of the geologic time scale. Calibrations of a time scale must ultimately be based on the application of meaningful isotopic ages to the succession of polarity intervals and geologic stages. A geochronologic scheme is thus an integration of several methodologies. It makes use of the best attributes of seafloor-spreading history (that is, the pattern of seafloor magnetic anomalies), magnetostratigraphy, and biostratigraphy in the application of relevant isotopic ages to derive a high-resolution and internally consistent time scale. The recent application of cyclical components driven by astronomical phenomena into the stratigraphic record, such as lithological couplets of marl and chalks as well as fluctuations in the ratios and percentages of fossil taxa, has resulted in fine-tuning the geologic time scale to a resolution of about 5,000 years in the late Neogene.

Micropaleontologists have created a number of zones based on the regional distribution of calcareous plankton (foraminiferans and nannoplankton) and those of the siliceous variety (radiolarians and diatoms), making it possible to correlate sediments from the high northern to high southern latitudes by way of the equatorial region. The resulting high-resolution zonal biostratigraphy and its calibration to an integrated geochronology provide the framework in which a true historical geology has become feasible.

CHAPTER 3

THE PALEOGENE PERIOD

The Paleogene, or Palaeogene, Period is the oldest of the three stratigraphic divisions of the Cenozoic Era. It spans the interval between 65.5 million and 23 million years ago. Paleogene is Greek meaning "ancient-born" and includes the Paleocene Epoch (65.5 million to 55.8 million years ago), the Eocene Epoch (55.8 million to 33.9 million years ago), and the Oligocene Epoch (33.9 million to 23 million years ago). The term Paleogene was devised in Europe to emphasize the similarity of marine fossils found in rocks of the first three Cenozoic epochs, as opposed to the later fossils of the Neogene Period (23 million to 2.6 million years ago) and the Quaternary Period (2.6 million years ago to the present). In North America, the Cenozoic has traditionally been divided only into the Tertiary Period (65.5 million to 2.6 million years ago) and the Quaternary Period; however, the Tertiary Period was officially replaced by the Paleogene and Neogene periods in 2008.

THE PALEOCENE EPOCH

The Paleocene, or Palaeocene, Epoch is the first major worldwide division of rocks and time of the Paleogene Period. It spans the interval between 65.5 million and 55.8 million years ago. The Paleocene Epoch was preceded by the Cretaceous Period and was followed by the Eocene Epoch. The Paleocene is subdivided into three ages and their corresponding rock stages: the Danian, Selandian, and Thanetian.

Marine rocks of Paleocene age are relatively limited in occurrence, and as a consequence much of the information about this epoch comes from terrestrial deposits. The most complete picture of Paleocene terrestrial life and environments is afforded by the rock record of North America. Elsewhere, Paleocene animals, especially mammals, are lacking or rare or are only of late Paleocene age. Prominent faunal remains of the late Paleocene Epoch are known from the regions of Cernay, France; Gashato, Mongolia; and the Chico River of Patagonian Argentina.

The North American climate during the Paleocene Epoch was characterized by a general warming trend with little or no frost. Seasonal variations probably can best be described as alternations of dry and wet seasons.

One of the most striking features of vertebrate life in the Paleocene Epoch was the complete absence of dinosaurs and other reptilian groups that were dominant during the preceding Cretaceous Period. Another salient feature was the rapid proliferation and evolution of mammals. Paleocene mammals included representatives of many groups or orders that still exist today, but the Paleocene forms were mostly archaic (that is, descended from yet earlier forms) or highly specialized. Paleocene mammals included Cretaceous species such as opossum-like marsupials and, especially, the archaic and unusual multituberculates—herbivorous animals that had teeth similar in some respects to those of the later, more advanced rodents. The condylarths, hoofed animals that were crucial members of the Paleocene animal kingdom, included forms that were evolving toward herbivorousness while still retaining insectivorous-carnivorous traits of their Cretaceous ancestors. Primates became more abundant in the middle Paleocene. They displayed characteristics intermediate between the insectivores and the lemurs, especially in their dental anatomy.

Late in the Paleocene, mammalian evolution showed a trend toward larger forms and more varied assemblages. Primitive mammalian carnivores—notably the creodonts (a group of catlike and doglike animals)—appeared, as did large herbivores, ancestral rodents, and the first known supposed primates. The Gashato fauna from Mongolia contains the remains of the earliest known hare (*Eurymylus*), and among Paleocene mammal remains from South America are many early representatives of animals that became dominant in subsequent epochs of the Paleogene Period.

Life in the early Paleocene oceans took hundreds of thousands to millions of years to recover from the mass extinction event at the end of the Cretaceous Period, but by Late Paleocene times many groups of marine invertebrate animals had diversified considerably, including mollusks and plankton. Highly fossiliferous marine sediments from the Upper Paleocene are well known along the Gulf and Atlantic coastal plains of North America.

DANIAN STAGE

The Danian Stage is the lowermost and oldest division of Paleocene rocks, corresponding to all rocks deposited worldwide during the Danian Age (65.5 million to 61.1 million years ago) of the Paleogene Period (65.5 million to 23 million years ago). This interval is named for exposures in Denmark, in which great quantities of Danian limestones are exposed and quarried.

The Global Stratotype Section and Point (GSSP), ratified by the International Commission on Stratigraphy (ICS) in 1991 and located 7 km (4 miles) west of the town of El-Kef, Tun., marks the base of this stage and thus the base of both the Paleogene Period and Cenozoic Era. The lower boundary of the Danian Stage also coincides with the Cretaceous–Paleogene (K–P) boundary. The upper boundary of the Danian coincides with the top of the zone of the foraminiferans (pseudopod-using unicellular organisms protected by a test or shell) *Praemurcia uncinata* and *Morozovella angulata* and the first appearance of *Globoconusa conusa*. The Danian Stage lies above the Maastrichtian Stage of the Cretaceous Period and precedes the Selandian Stage of the Paleogene.

SELANDIAN STAGE

The Selandian, or Seelandian, Stage is the second-oldest division of Paleocene rocks, representing all rocks deposited worldwide during the Selandian Age (61.1 million to 58.7 million years ago) of the Paleogene Period (65.5 million to 23 million years ago). It is named for marine strata in the Seeland region of Denmark.

The lower boundary of the Selandian Stage is approximately coincident with the first appearance of the foraminiferan (pseudopod-using unicellular organism protected by a test or shell) *Morozovella angulata*. The upper boundary of the Selandian Stage lies within the zone of the dinoflagellate (single-celled, aquatic organism with two dissimilar flagellae and exhibiting traits of both plants and animals) microfossil *Alisocysta margarita*. The Selandian Stage overlies the Danian Stage and underlies the Thanetian Stage.

THANETIAN STAGE

The Thanetian Stage is the uppermost division of Paleocene rocks, embodying all rocks deposited worldwide during the Thanetian Age (58.7 million to 55.8 million years ago) of the Paleogene Period (65.5 million to 23 million years ago). The Thanetian Stage is named for the Thanet Sands, Isle of Thanet, Kent, Eng.

The lower boundary of the Thanetian Stage is coincident with the first occurrence of the calcareous nannoplankton (a single-celled, photosynthetic organism with a shell made up of calcium carbonate plates called coccoliths) *Areoligeria gippingensis*. The upper boundary (equivalent to the boundary between the Paleocene and Eocene epochs) is coincident with the first appearance of the dinoflagellate (single-celled, aquatic organisms with two dissimilar flagellae and exhibiting traits of both plants and animals) *Apectodinium augustum*. The Thanetian Stage overlies the Selandian Stage and precedes the Ypresian Stage.

THE EOCENE EPOCH

The Eocene Epoch is the second of three major worldwide divisions of the Paleogene Period that began 55.8 million years ago and ended 33.9 million years ago. It follows the Paleocene Epoch and precedes the Oligocene Epoch. The Eocene is often divided into Early (55.8 million to 48.6 million years ago), Middle (48.6 million to 37.2 million years ago), and Late (37.2 million to 33.9 million years ago) epochs. The name Eocene is derived from the Greek *eos*, for "dawn," referring to the appearance and diversification of many modern groups of organisms, especially mammals and mollusks.

Eocene rocks have a worldwide distribution. The ICS has recognized several stages and their temporal equivalents (ages) on the basis of characteristic rocks and fossils: Ypresian, Lutetian, Bartonian, and Priabonian (from earliest to latest). Lower Eocene assemblages are poorly represented in both England and the Patagonian region of South America. Later Eocene vertebrate faunas are somewhat better developed in areas outside of North America.

It is in North America, especially the western United States, however, that the most abundant and extensive Eocene terrestrial vertebrate record exists. Eocene rocks were deposited in much the same regions as those of the preceding Paleocene Epoch. During the Eocene, climates were warm and humid. Temperate and subtropical forests were widespread, whereas grasslands were of limited extent. For example, the Eocene forests of Oregon were made up of trees and plants similar or identical to those now found in Central and South America.

During the Eocene, the vertebrates of North America and Europe were similar. Many genera existed in both regions, indicating that an interchange between the regions was possible. Early Eocene faunas mirrored those of the preceding Paleocene with the addition of newer types, but the archaic Paleocene groups gradually became extinct.

Among terrestrial vertebrates, the start of the Eocene is marked by the appearance of two new groups of animals: the perissodactyls, or odd-toed ungulates, and the artiodactyls, or even-toed ungulates. The perissodactyls include the horses, rhinoceroses, and tapirs; among the artiodactyls are the deer, cattle, and sheep. An early horse ancestor, the dawn horse, known in North America as *Eohippus*, is among the fossil perissodactyls found in the lower Eocene rocks of both North America and Europe. Artiodactyls, rare during the early Eocene, became abundant later in the epoch.

Archaic primate forms from the Paleocene Epoch declined during the Eocene as many of their ecological niches were usurped by the more efficient rodents. Vertebrate groups arising during the Middle Eocene were less widespread than those of the early Eocene. The resulting isolation allowed different evolutionary trends to occur in the ungulate groups of North America and Europe. By late in the Eocene Epoch this isolation had

Coryphodon, a genus of primitive hoofed mammals known from Late Paleocene and Early Eocene deposits. Restoration painting by Charles R. Knight, 1898. Courtesy of the American Museum of Natural History, New York

ceased, and North American and European groups once again came into contact with one another.

The Eocene Epoch marks the first appearance in the fossil record of the two completely marine mammal groups: cetaceans (whales, porpoises, and dolphins) and sirenians (akin to the modern manatees and dugongs). Similarly, the Eocene provides the first elephant-like animals and the early bats. In addition, gastropods (a class of mollusks containing snails, slugs, and limpets) underwent great diversification, and many bird orders that were in essence modern appeared during the Eocene.

YPRESIAN STAGE

The Ypresian Stage is the oldest division of Eocene rocks, representing all rocks deposited worldwide during the Ypresian Age (55.8 million to 48.6 million years ago) of the Paleogene Period. The Ypresian Stage is named for exposures in the region of Ypres, Bel.

The GSSP defining the lower boundary of this stage, ratified by the ICS in 2003, is located within the Dababiya Section approximately 25 km (16 miles) south of Luxor, Egypt. The lower boundary of the Ypresian Stage coincides with the base of the dinoflagellate (single-celled, aquatic organisms with two dissimilar flagellae and exhibiting traits of both plants and animals) *Apectodinium augustum*. The upper boundary matches the first occurrence of the foraminiferan (pseudopod-using unicellular organism protected by a test or shell) *Hantkenina nuttalli*. The Ypresian Stage precedes the Lutetian Stage and overlies the Thanetian Stage.

LUTETIAN STAGE

The second of four stages (in ascending order) subdividing Eocene rocks, the Lutetian Stage represents all rocks deposited worldwide during the Lutetian Age (48.6 million to 40.4 million years ago) of the Paleogene Period. The name of this stage is derived from Lutetia (the ancient Latin name for Paris), France, where rocks of this age are well-exposed.

The lower boundary of the Lutetian Stage coincides with the base of the zone of the foraminiferan (pseudopod-using unicellular organism protected by a test or shell) *Hantkenina nuttalli*. The Lutetian Stage overlies the Ypresian Stage and precedes the Bartonian Stage.

BARTONIAN STAGE

The third of four divisions (in ascending order) of Eocene rocks, the Bartonian Stage accounts for all rocks deposited worldwide during the Bartonian Age (40.4 million to 37.2 million years ago) of the Paleogene Period. The name of the stage is derived from the Barton Beds found between Highcliffe and Milford-on-Sea in Hampshire, England. The Bartonian is underlain by the Lutetian Stage and overlain by the Priabonian Stage.

PRIABONIAN STAGE

The Priabonian Stage is the uppermost division of Eocene rocks, corresponding to all rocks deposited worldwide during the Priabonian Age (37.2 million to 33.9 million years ago) of the Paleogene Period (65.5 million to 23 million years ago). The Priabonian Stage is named for Priabona in the Vicenza province of northern Italy.

The lower boundary of the Priabonian Stage coincides with the first appearance of the calcareous nannoplankton (a single-celled, photosynthetic organism with a shell made up of calcium carbonate plates called coccoliths) *Chiasmolithus oamaruensis*. The upper boundary matches the extinction level of the foraminiferan (pseudopod-using unicellular organism protected by a test or shell) *Turborotalia cerroazulensis*. The Priabonian Stage overlies the Bartonian Stage and underlies the Rupelian Stage.

THE OLIGOCENE EPOCH

The Oligocene Epoch is the third and last major worldwide division of the Paleogene Period (65.5 million to 23 million years ago), spanning the interval between 33.9

million to 23 million years ago. The Oligocene Epoch is subdivided into two ages and their corresponding rock stages: the Rupelian and the Chattian. It followed the Eocene Epoch and was succeeded by the Miocene Epoch, the first epoch of the Neogene Period. The term Oligocene is derived from Greek and means the "epoch of few recent forms," referring to the sparseness of the number of modern animals that originated during that time.

In western Europe the beginning of the Oligocene was marked by an invasion of the sea that brought with it new mollusks characteristic of the epoch. Marine conditions did not exist for long, however, and brackish and freshwater conditions soon prevailed. This cycle of marine transgression, followed by the establishment of brackish and then freshwater environments, was repeated during the Oligocene. Sediments on the floor of the ancient Tethyan Sea, which covered part of Eurasia during the Oligocene, were deformed early in the development of the European Alps.

Oligocene climates appear to have been temperate, and many regions enjoyed subtropical climatic conditions. Grasslands expanded and forested regions dwindled during this time, while tropical vegetation flourished along the borders of the Tethyan Sea. Warm, swampy conditions prevailed over much of what is now Germany, and extensive deposits of lignite coal were formed.

A prominent group of Oligocene marine organisms were the foraminiferans, protists similar to amoebas but bearing a complex, often calcareous test, or shell. Among the especially prominent foraminiferans were the nummulites (large, lens-shaped foraminiferans), and other marine forms were essentially modern in aspect. Terrestrial invertebrate life was abundant and diverse. Stream and lake deposits on the Isle of Wight in England contain the remains, often well preserved, of termites and other insects. In the Baltic, many forms of Oligocene insects, including butterflies, bees, ants, and spiders, are preserved in amber.

Oligocene terrestrial vertebrate faunas are diverse and abundant and are known from North America, Europe, Africa, and Asia. The vertebrates of the northern continents possess an essentially modern aspect that is more a result of the extinction of archaic vertebrates at the close of the Eocene Epoch than the appearance of new forms. The similarities between the various early Oligocene vertebrate faunas of the northern continents suggests a relatively free interchange of animals, but later Oligocene faunas show a greater degree of provincialism. Early pigs and peccaries first appeared in Europe during the early Oligocene and reached North America late in the epoch. Bats became more widespread during the Oligocene and at least locally abundant. Their droppings in caves contributed to the formation of extensive phosphate deposits that are now economically significant in many areas.

Throughout the epoch, modern groups of carnivores and herbivores became diverse and abundant. The largest land mammal of all time, *Indricotherium* (a sort of giant hornless rhinoceros),

Indricotherium, *detail of a restoration painting by Charles R. Knight.* Courtesy of the American Museum of Natural History, New York

is known from Asia, and the first mastodons are known from Egypt. In North America, primitive horses were evolving, including three-toed forms such as *Mesohippus* and *Miohippus*. Primitive beavers also appeared late in the Oligocene.

The earliest apelike form, *Parapithecus*, is known from Oligocene deposits in Egypt, which also have yielded remains of several kinds of Old World monkeys. The earliest New World monkeys are known from late Oligocene deposits in South America. During the Oligocene, South America was isolated from Central and North America, and a unique mammalian fauna developed there. Remarkably, many South American mammals of the Oligocene exhibit extreme parallelism in adaptation to forms that are found elsewhere in the world and to which they are not closely related.

RUPELIAN STAGE

The lowermost division of Oligocene rocks, the Rupelian Stage corresponds to all rocks deposited worldwide during the Rupelian Age (33.9 million to 28.4 million years ago) of the Paleogene Period. It is named for exposures studied along the Rupel, a tributary of the Scheldt River in Belgium.

The GSSP defining the lower boundary of this stage, ratified by the ICS in 1992, is located in the Massignano section, which lies in a quarry about 10 km (6 miles) southeast of Ancona, Italy. This lower boundary matches the extinction zone of the foraminiferan (pseudopod-using unicellular organism protected by a test or shell) genera *Hantkenina* and *Cribrohantkenina*. The upper boundary is located near the extinction level of the foraminiferan *Chiloguembelina*. The Rupelian Stage overlies the Priabonian Stage and underlies the Chattian Stage.

CHATTIAN STAGE

The Chattian Stage is the uppermost and latest division of Oligocene rocks, embodying all rocks deposited world-wide during the Chattian Age (28.4 million to 23 million years ago) of the Paleogene Period. The Chattian Stage is named for the Chatti, an ancient tribe that inhabited the Cassel region of northern Germany.

The lower boundary of the Chattian Stage coincides with the top of the zone of the calcareous nannofossil (remains of ocean-dwelling golden-brown algae) *Chiloguembelina*. The upper boundary is nearly coincident with the top of the zone of the foraminiferan (pseudopod-using unicellular organism protected by a test or shell) *Globorotalia kugleri*. The Chattian overlies the Rupelian Stage of the Paleogene System and directly underlies the Aquitanian Stage of the Neogene System.

SIGNIFICANT LIFE-FORMS OF THE PALEOGENE PERIOD

Mammals emerged as the dominant forms of life during the Paleogene Period. Some of these forms were quite large. The *Indricotherium*, the largest mammal that ever existed, grew to more than 8 metres (26 feet) long. Other Paleogene mammals found as fossils were notable in that they represent close relatives of the ancestors of modern mammalian groups. For example, the dawn horse (*Hyracotherium*) is thought to be related to the progenitor of the perissodactyls, the odd-toed hoofed mammals. Primitive primates, such as *Notharctus*, and primitive whales, such as *Basilosaurus*, also emerged during Paleogene times.

Arsinoitherium

Arsinoitherium is a genus of extinct large, primitive, hoofed mammals found as fossils in Egypt in deposits from the Eocene Epoch (55.8 million to 33.9 million years ago) and elsewhere in deposits from the Oligocene Epoch (33.9 million to 23 million years ago). The animal, probably a swamp dweller, reached a length of about 3.5 metres (11 feet) and was about the size of a large rhinoceros. It carried an enormous pair of horns on the nasal bones and an additional, smaller pair of horns on the frontal bones. Relatives are known from Egypt to Southeast Asia. This animal is also considered to be distantly related to proboscideans (elephants and their kin).

Barylambda

Barylambda was an extinct genus of unusual and aberrant mammals found as North American fossils in deposits in the late Paleocene Epoch (58.7 million to 55.8 million years ago). Although *Barylambda* was among the largest animals of its time, 2.5 metres (about 8 feet) long, its skull was relatively small and short. It had an unusually massive body and legs and a thick tail that may have been used as a support, allowing the animal to raise itself on its hind legs. Its feet were short and broad, with five digits. *Barylambda* retained clavicles, or collarbones, a feature that is considered primitive in hoofed mammals. *Barylambda* likely fed on plants that were rather soft and easily chewed.

Basilosaurus

Basilosaurus, which is also called *Zeuglodon*, is an extinct genus of primitive whales of the family Basilosauridae (suborder Archaeoceti) found in Middle and Late Eocene rocks in North America and northern Africa. *Basilosaurus* had primitive dentition and skull architecture, and the rest of the slender, elongated skeleton was well adapted to aquatic life. It grew to a length of about 21 metres (about 70 feet), with the skull alone as much as 1.5 metres (5 feet) long. *Basilosaurus* was common throughout late Eocene seas.

BORHYAENIDAE

A family of extinct South American marsupial mammals occurring from the Early Paleocene Epoch into the Early Pliocene (from about 63.5 to 5 million years ago), Borhyaenidae is named for the genus *Borhyaena*. *Borhyaena* contains the hyena-like specimens of this family found in early Miocene rocks of Argentina (23 million years old). Members of this genus had large skulls and heavy crushing teeth. Not all borhyaenids were hyenoid, however. *Thylacosmilus* was a Pliocene-aged marsupial counterpart of the sabre-toothed tiger. Many other forms were wolf-like and foxlike.

BRONTOTHERE

Brontotheres (members of the extinct genus *Brontotherium*) were large, hoofed, herbivorous mammals found as fossils in North American deposits of the Oligocene Epoch. *Brontotherium* is representative of the titanotheres, large perissodactyls that share a common ancestry with the horse. Indeed, the titanotheres probably derived from a form that was similar to the dawn horse (*Hyracotherium*). Adult brontotheres stood up to 2.5 metres (about 8 feet) high at the shoulder. Although the skull was massive and long, the brain was smaller than the brains of most living hoofed mammals. A pair of large horns at the front of the animal's skull was united at their base but split toward their apex. Brontotheres had large teeth, but they were primitive and adapted to consuming soft vegetation.

CORYPHODON

Coryphodon was a genus of extinct primitive hoofed mammals known from Late Paleocene and Early Eocene deposits (those that date from about 63.5 to 52 million years ago) in North America and Early Eocene deposits in Europe and eastern Asia (the Paleocene epoch, which preceded the Eocene epoch, ended about 55.8 million years ago). *Coryphodon,* representative of an archaic group, the pantodonts, was a robust animal about as large as a modern tapir. The skeleton was heavy and the limbs strongly constructed to support the animal's bulk. The feet were broad and had five toes. Its skull was broad, relatively flat, and lacked horns or other protuberances, except in the back or occipital region, where powerful neck muscles were attached. *Coryphodon* had large upper canines. The presence of 44 teeth represents the primitive mammalian condition. *Coryphodon* was not a swift animal. It probably was a browser, feeding much like the modern tapirs.

DAWN HORSE

The dawn horse, genus *Hyracotherium*, was a member of an extinct group of horses that flourished in North America and Europe during the early part of the Eocene Epoch. Even though these animals are more commonly known as *Eohippus*, a name given by the American paleontologist Othniel Charles Marsh, they are properly placed in the genus *Hyracotherium*, the name given earlier by British paleontologist Richard Owen.

The dawn horse was a form close to the common ancestry of all the odd-toed hoofed mammals, the

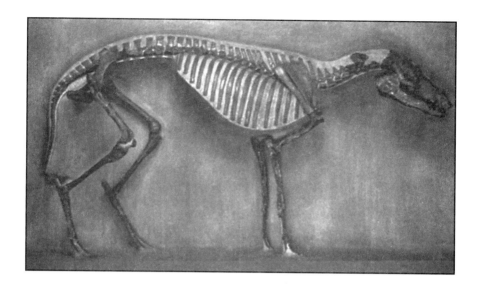

Dawn horse (Hyracotherium*) skeleton.* Courtesy of the American Museum of Natural History, New York

perissodactyls. It stood thirty to sixty cm (1–2 feet) high at the shoulder, depending on the species. Because its hind legs were longer than its forelegs, *Hyracotherium* was adapted to running and probably relied heavily on running to escape predators. The body was lightly constructed and raised well off the ground, its slender limbs supported by toes held in an almost vertical position. Although four toes were present on the front feet and three on the hind feet, all were functionally three-toed, and each toe ended in a small hoof.

The skull of *Hyracotherium* varied in length. Some species had a relatively short face, but in others the face was long and more horselike. The incisors of *Hyracotherium* were small, and the cheek teeth had low crowns, which indicated the animal was a browser that fed on leaves rather than grass. The dawn horse was succeeded by *Orohippus*, which differed from *Hyracotherium* primarily in dentition.

Diatryma

Diatryma is an extinct genus of giant flightless birds found as fossils in Early Eocene rocks in North America and Europe. *Diatryma* grew to a height of about 2 ¼ metres (7 feet). Its small wings were not used for flight, but its legs were massively constructed, likely making *Diatryma* a strong and rapid runner. Its large head supported a powerful beak. *Diatryma* was an active predator, probably feeding on the small mammals.

In South America a similarly adapted group is characterized by the unrelated genus *Phorusrhacos*, common during the Miocene Epoch (between 23 million and 5.3 million years ago). It was about 1 ½ metres (5 feet) in height and also had weakly developed wings, strong legs, a large head, and a mighty beak.

Hyaenodon

An extinct genus of carnivorous mammals, *Hyaenodon* first appeared in the fossil record about 42 million years ago during the middle of the Eocene Epoch and persisted until about 25 million years ago near the end of the Oligocene Epoch. The genus, in the order Creodonta, contained about 30 species. *Hyaenodon* was a large and efficient predator. Its skull was long and narrow, with large, catlike teeth. The body of *Hyaenodon* was more doglike, however, and the animal would have been similar to the recently extinct Tasmanian wolf, *Thylacinus*.

Indricotherium

Indricotherium (also called *Paraceratherium*, formerly *Baluchitherium*) is a genus of giant browsing perissodactyls found as fossils in Asian deposits of the Late Oligocene

Depiction of the extinct genus. Hyaenodon. Encyclopædia Britannica, Inc.

and Early Miocene epochs (30 to 16.6 million years ago). *Indricotherium*, a hornless relation of the modern rhinoceros, was the largest land mammal that ever existed. It stood about 5.5 metres (18 feet) high at the shoulder, was 8 metres (26 feet) long, and weighed approximately 30 tons, which is more than four times the weight of the modern elephant. With relatively long front legs and a long neck, *Indricotherium* probably browsed on the leaves and tree branches. Its limbs were massive and strongly constructed. Its skull, small in proportion to its body, was more than 1.2 metres (4 feet) long.

LITOPTERN

Litopterns are any of various extinct hoofed mammals belonging to the order Litopterna. They first appeared in the Paleocene Epoch and died out during the Pleistocene Epoch. The order was restricted to South America, but in many ways, the evolution of the litopterns paralleled that of hoofed mammals in the Northern Hemisphere. Two distinct lineages of litoptern evolution are discernible in the fossil record.

One line of litopterns, the proterotheres, strongly resembled horses. Their limbs were modified for running and also had special features for locking their knees, allowing them to stand for long periods of time. The proterothere skull was long and low and contained cheek teeth resembling those of deer. Proterotheres became extinct in the Pliocene Epoch (5.3 million to 2.6 million years ago), about the time that true horses appeared in South America.

The other litoptern group, the macrauchenids, resembled camels. The nasal opening was set high on the skull, which probably supported a short proboscis, or trunk. Some of the macrauchenids survived the intrusion of more advanced mammals from North America and persisted well into the Pleistocene Epoch.

MESOHIPPUS

Mesohippus is a genus of extinct early and middle Oligocene horses. Members of the genus are commonly found as fossils in the rocks of the Badlands region of South Dakota, U.S. *Mesohippus* was the first of the three-toed horses and, although only the size of a modern collie dog, was horselike in appearance. Still a browsing form, *Mesohippus* teeth were unsuited to the grazing adopted by later, more advanced horses. *Mesohippus* gave rise to the next stage in horse evolution, the genus *Miohippus,* a larger form that was common in the late Oligocene (28.4 to 23 million years ago).

MIACIS

Miacis is a genus of extinct carnivores found as fossils in deposits of the Late Paleocene Epoch to the late Eocene

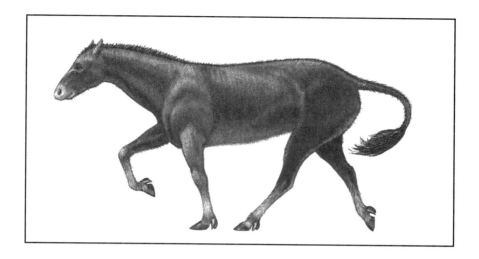

Mesohippus. Encyclopædia Britannica, Inc.

Epoch in North America and of the Late Eocene Epoch in
Europe and Asia. It is representative of a group of early
carnivores, the miacids, that were the ancestors of modern caniforms: the canids (that is, the dogs, coyotes,
wolves, foxes, and jackals) and a large group made up of
the bear, raccoon, and weasel families. Miacids were quite
diverse, with body masses that ranged from about 1 to 7 kg
(2.2 to 15.4 pounds). It is probable that the earliest members of the genus were at least partly arboreal (tree
dwelling), capable of reversing their hind feet much as
squirrels do when they climb. The hind limbs were longer
than the forelimbs, and the pelvis was very doglike in form
and structure. Some specialized traits are present in the
vertebrae. *Miacis* was probably a forest dweller that preyed
upon smaller animals. Some species were similar to civets
in form, whereas others bore a resemblance to kinkajous.

Miacis, *a carnivorous mammal that lived during the Paleocene and Eocene epochs.* Encyclopædia Britannica, Inc.

MIOHIPPUS

A genus of extinct horses that originated in North America during the Late Eocene Epoch (37.2 to 33.9 million years ago), *Miohippus* evolved from the earlier genus *Mesohippus*; however, the former was larger and had a more-derived dentition than the latter. The number of toes in *Miohippus* was reduced to three, which enabled it to run considerably faster than its five-toed ancestors. *Miohippus* persisted into the Miocene Epoch side by side with its more horse-like one-toed relatives.

MOERITHERIUM

Moeritherium is an extinct genus of primitive mammals that represent an early stage in the evolution of elephants. Its fossils are found in deposits dated to the Eocene Epoch and the early part of the Oligocene Epoch in northern

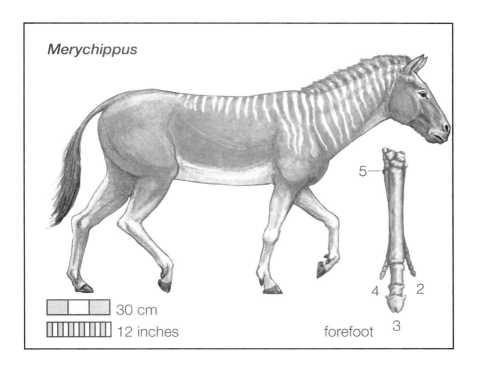

Merychippus

5—

4 2

3

30 cm

12 inches   forefoot

The ancestral horse Miohippus, *in an artist's conception. Existing toe bones of the forefoot are numbered outward from the centre of the body.* Encyclopædia Britannica, Inc.

Africa. *Moeritherium* did not resemble living elephants. It was about as large as a tapir, with short, strong legs, a relatively long body, and a short tail. The feet of *Moeritherium* were broad and terminated in flat-hoofed toes. The skull and cheekbone were long, eyes were set rather far forward, and nasal openings were located on the upper side of the skull. It is unlikely that an elephantine trunk was present. At most, *Moeritherium* had a short, flexible proboscis much like that of tapirs. The front incisors were strongly developed in upper and lower jaws, and they represent a stage in the development of the familiar elephant tusks. Strong neck muscles were attached to the broad back end of the skull. *Moeritherium* inhabited marshy regions and was at least partly aquatic, feeding on vegetation.

NOTHARCTUS

Notharctus is an extinct genus of small primates (family Adapidae) that shares many similarities with modern lemurs, but its exact relationship to lemurs is controversial. The genus is well known from complete fossil remains found in Europe and North America in early Eocene deposits dated to about 54 million years ago.

The skull of *Notharctus* was about 5 cm (2 inches) long, with a prominent muzzle. It had long canine teeth and four premolars, which differentiate it from modern lemurs. The legs and tail were long and slim. The first digit

Notharctus, *an extinct mammal genus*. Encyclopædia Britannica, Inc.

of the feet and hands was set off from the rest and may have been opposable. *Notharctus* was probably an agile climber, and during the Eocene, it inhabited the dense subtropical forests that flourished over much of North America and Eurasia. *Notharctus* and its close relatives became extinct by the end of the Eocene Epoch. Other more modern lemurs survived in tropical forests elsewhere and became particularly successful on Madagascar, where they remained relatively free from competition.

NOTOUNGULATA

Notoungulata is an extinct group of hoofed mammals found as fossils, mostly in South America, but the oldest forms seem to have originated in East Asia. Notoungulates lived from the late Paleocene Epoch to the early part of the Pleistocene Epoch and were most diverse during the Miocene Epoch. By the Pliocene Epoch their numbers and diversity were reduced, perhaps owing to changes in climate and geography. In South America, notoungulates evolved and diversified in isolation until they became extinct after the land connection between North and South America was reestablished about 3.5 million years ago.

In their time, the notoungulates included a variety of hoofed animals whose development paralleled the evolution of more advanced forms elsewhere. One group, the toxodonts, was clumsily built and rather massive. Members of the genus *Toxodon* stood about 1.5 metres (5 feet) high at the shoulder. Other notoungulates developed along lines similar to rabbits and rodents.

NUMMULITES

Nummulites are any of the thousands of extinct species of relatively large, lens-shaped foraminifers (single-celled marine organisms) that were abundant during the Paleogene and Neogene periods (65.5 million to 2.6 million years ago). *Nummulite* was particularly prominent during the Eocene Epoch, and limestone of this age that occurs in the Sahara is called nummulite limestone in reference to the great abundance of its contained fossil nummulites.

OLIVE SHELL

Marine snails that constitute the family Olividae (subclass Prosobranchia of the class Gastropoda) are known as olive shells. Fossils of the genus *Oliva* are common from the Eocene Epoch to the present. The shell, which is distinctive and easily recognizable, has a pointed apex and rapidly expands outward to the main body whorl. It is oval in shape, with a long and narrow aperture, and possesses an agatelike sheen and fine markings. Folds are developed on the end of the body whorl in a characteristic pattern.

Olives burrow in sandy bottoms. Common in southeastern American waters is the lettered olive (*Oliva sayana*), about 6 cm (2.5 inches) long. Abundant in the Indo-Pacific region is the 8-centimetre (3-inch) orange-mouthed olive (*O. sericea*).

PHENACODUS

An extinct genus of mammals known from fossils of the late Paleocene and early Eocene epochs of North America and Europe, *Phenacodus* is representative of early ungulates, or hoofed mammals. It had five toes and a digitigrade stance like that of a dog, with many specializations for running. The structure and dentition of *Phenacodus* suggest that it was fairly omnivorous. Although the canine

Phenacodus, *restoration painting by Charles R. Knight, 1898.* Courtesy of the American Museum of Natural History, New York

teeth were large and well developed, the cheek teeth were at least partly adapted to eating plants.

PTILODUS

Ptilodus is an extinct genus of mammals found as fossils in deposits dated to the Paleocene Epoch of North America. *Ptilodus* was a multituberculate, a group of rodentlike mammals that were once the dominant herbivores and granivores in terrestrial ecosystems. The teeth of *Ptilodus* included long rodentlike incisors, bladelike shearing teeth with striations, and molars with parallel rows of cusps. The palate had large spaces, and powerful chewing muscles were attached to the lower jaw.

Ptilodus

Ptilodus, *extinct genus of mammal resembling a squirrel.* Encyclopædia Britannica, Inc.

SABRE-TOOTHED CATS

Sabre-toothed cats are any of the extinct catlike carnivores belonging to either the extinct family Nimravidae or the subfamily Machairodontinae of the cat family (Felidae). Named for the pair of elongated, bladelike canine teeth in their upper jaw, they are often called sabre-toothed tigers or sabre-toothed lions, however, the modern lion and tiger are true cats of the subfamily Felinae.

Sabre-toothed cats existed from the Eocene through the Pleistocene Epoch (55.8 million to 11,700 years ago). According to the fossil record, the Nimravidae were extant from about 37 million to about 7 million years ago. Only distantly related to felids, they include the genera *Hoplophoneus*, *Nimravus*, *Dinictis*, and *Barbourofelis*. The Machairodontinae, extant from about 12 million to less than 10,000 years ago, include the more familiar *Smilodon* as well as *Homotherium* and *Meganteron*. Sabre-toothed cats roamed North America and Europe throughout the Miocene and Pliocene epochs (23 million to 2.6 million years ago). By Pliocene times, they had spread to Asia and

Africa. During the Pleistocene, sabre-toothed cats were also present in South America.

The most widely known genus of sabre-toothed cats is *Smilodon*. A large, short-limbed cat that lived in North and South America during the Pleistocene Epoch, it was about the size of the modern African lion (*Panthera leo*) and represents the peak of sabre-tooth evolution. Its immense upper canine teeth, up to 20 cm (8 inches) long, were probably used for stabbing and slashing attacks, possibly on large herbivores such as the mastodon. Several physical adaptations of *Smilodon* suggest such a hunting technique: its skull was modified to accommodate the attachment of strong neck muscles for bringing the head down, the lower canines were reduced, and the jaw could be opened to about a 90° angle to free the upper canines for action. Its molars formed shearing blades with no trace of grinding surfaces. The bones of many *Smilodon* specimens have been recovered from the La Brea Tar Pits, in Los Angeles, Calif., where the cats were apparently mired in the tar as they preyed on other trapped animals.

The extinction pattern of the last of the sabre-toothed cats closely followed that of the mastodons. As those elephant-like animals became extinct in the Old World during the late Pliocene, sabre-toothed cats died out also. In North and South America, however, where mastodons persisted throughout the Pleistocene, sabre-toothed cats continued successfully to the end of the epoch.

TAENIODONT

Taeniodonts are members of an extinct suborder (Taeniodonta) of mammals that lived in North America throughout the Paleocene Epoch and into the middle of the Eocene Epoch (that is, about 65.5 million to 43 million years ago). The taeniodont is part of the larger mammalian order Cimolesta, a diverse group ranging from small insectivorous types to large herbivores. Taeniodonts are distinguished by high-crowned teeth extending far into the skull.

The single known family, Stylinodontidae, is made up of two subfamilies, Conoryctinae and Stylinodontinae. The Conoryctinae were rather generalized forms with no special peculiarities. During the Paleocene, they gradually increased from the size of an opossum to that of a small bear; however, they did not survive the close of the Paleocene Epoch. The Stylinodontinae, by contrast, became progressively more specialized. Stylinodonts culminated in forms with extremely short and broad skulls; deep, massively built lower jaws; rootless teeth; and limbs tipped by very large, long claws that were used for either grasping or digging. The animals' canine teeth were extremely large and specialized for gnawing. Together, the claws and teeth suggest adaptation to a specialized diet, the nature of which remains unknown.

TITANOTHERE

Titanotheres belong to an extinct group of large-hoofed mammals that originated in Asia or North America during the early Eocene Epoch (some 50 million years ago) and became extinct during the middle of the Oligocene Epoch (some 28 million years ago). Most were large and fed mainly on soft vegetation. Their skulls were massive and frequently adorned with large bony protuberances covered in skin that may have been used in intraspecific combat or as defensive weapons against predators. The bodies were bulky with strong, pillarlike limbs. The remains of titanotheres are abundant in the geologic record, and the different forms must have been locally numerous. It is possible that they moved about in herds.

UINTATHERIUM

Uintatherium is a genus of large, extinct, hoofed mammals found as fossils in North America and Asia in terrestrial deposits that date from the middle of the Eocene Epoch. The size of a modern rhinoceros, *Uintatherium* was among the largest animals of its time. The limbs were strongly constructed to support the massive body. Three pairs of bony growths, or protuberances, were present on the skull, and the anterior pair may have supported prominent horns. The teeth were also distinctive: males of the genus possessed large, powerful canines; incisors were absent in the upper jaw but present in a reduced state in the lower; and the upper molars were characterized by V-shaped crests.

VENERICARDIA

Venericardia is a genus of pelecypods (clams) abundant during the Eocene Epoch. The shell, composed of two halves (valves), is distinctive in form and generally large. Transverse ribs radiate from the apex of the valves and are broken by a series of concentric growth rings. Internally, the valves are marked by distinctive nodes along the edge and thickenings that form raised bars at the apex, forming the surfaces along which the valves articulate.

Venericardia divergens. Courtesy of the Buffalo Museum of Science, Buffalo, N.Y. Encyclopædia Britannica, Inc.

CHAPTER 4
THE NEOGENE PERIOD

The Neogene Period is the second of three divisions of the Cenozoic Era. The Neogene Period encompasses the interval between 23 million and 2.6 million years ago and includes the Miocene (23 million to 5.3 million years ago) and the Pliocene (5.3 million to 2.6 million years ago) epochs. The Neogene, which means "new born," was designated as such to emphasize that the marine and terrestrial fossils found in the strata of this time were more closely related to each other than to those of the preceding period, called the Paleogene (65.5 million to 23 million years ago). The term Neogene is widely used in Europe as a geologic division, and it is increasingly employed in North America, where the Cenozoic Era has traditionally been divided into the Tertiary Period (65.5 million to 2.6 million years ago) and the Quaternary Period (2.6 million years ago to the present).

THE MIOCENE EPOCH

The Miocene Epoch is the earliest major worldwide division of the Neogene Period that extended from 23 million to 5.3 million years ago. It is often divided into the Early Miocene Epoch (23 million to 16 million years ago), the Middle Miocene Epoch (16 million to 11.6 million years ago), and the Late Miocene Epoch (11.6 million to 5.3 million years ago). The Miocene may also be divided into six ages and their corresponding rock stages: from oldest to youngest these ages or stages are the Aquitanian, Burdigalian, Langhian, Serravallian, Tortonian, and

Messinian. The Miocene followed the Oligocene Epoch of the Paleogene Period and was succeeded by the Pliocene Epoch.

Important Miocene deposits are found in North and South America, southern Europe, India, Mongolia, East Africa, and Pakistan. Both marine and terrestrial environments are represented in the Miocene stratigraphic record. The record of terrestrial life is extensive and varied, providing a rather complete view of the development of vertebrates, especially mammals.

During the Miocene, land-dwelling mammals were essentially modern; many archaic groups were extinct by the end of the preceding Oligocene, and fully half of the mammalian families known today are present in the Miocene record. In the Northern Hemisphere, some interchange of faunas occurred between the Old and New Worlds. Interchange was also possible between Africa and Eurasia, but South America and Australia remained isolated. During the Miocene, horse evolution occurred mainly in North America. Forms such as *Parahippus*, *Miohippus* (a form carried over from the preceding Oligocene Epoch), *Anchitherium*, *Hypohippus*, *Pliohippus*, and *Merychippus* are genera that represent great diversification and development. Also, the first dogs and bears

Moropus, *an extinct genus of the chalicotheres (ungulates with claws instead of hooves) related to the horse. Fossil remains are found in Miocene deposits of North America and Asia.* Courtesy of the American Museum of Natural History, New York

appeared, with the first emergence of the bear-dog *Hemicyon* occurring close to the origin of the bears. The first hyenas, springing from primitive civets, appeared in the Miocene, as did the first sabre-toothed cats of the subfamily Machairodontinae. Primitive antelope, deer, and giraffes appeared in Eurasia during the Miocene. Ancestors of the modern elephants, which during the preceding Oligocene seem to have been limited to Africa, appear to have spread to the Eurasian continent during the Miocene and became more diverse.

In Argentina the Santa Cruz Formation of Middle Miocene time provides an excellent record of the unusual Miocene fauna of South America. Marsupial carnivores, aberrant endentates (mammals resembling anteaters, armadillos, and sloths), litopterns (hoofed mammals similar to horses and camels), and toxodonts (mammals with long, curved incisors) are among the odd groups represented. These forms were able to evolve because of South America's isolation from other regions. The evolution of the South American monkeys was also under way during the Miocene.

By the end of the Miocene Epoch, almost all the modern groups of whales had appeared, as had the early seals and walruses. Birds such as herons, rails, ducks, eagles, hawks, crows, sparrows, pheasants, owls, and partridges were present in Europe, where the uplifting of the Alps continued through Miocene time.

The Miocene Epoch is also crucial to primate evolution. The last primate to occur in the fossil record of North America, a tarsier-like creature, is known in the United States. Elsewhere, the higher primates, especially the apes, underwent a great deal of evolution. The fossil evidence seems to indicate that advanced primates, including apes, were present in southern Europe. An early gibbon,

Pliopithecus, as well as the dryopithecines, a group of advanced humanlike apes that probably represent the stock from which modern apes and humans originated, are found in Miocene rocks of Europe. The dryopithecines also are present in the Miocene of Africa, the region where humanlike forms as well as modern humans probably originated.

In the oceans, the Miocene was a time of changing circulation patterns, probably a result of global cooling. Patterns of oceanic nutrient distribution changed, leading to increased productivity in some regions and decreased productivity in others. The Miocene was a time of accelerated evolution among marine plankton and mollusks, with many groups showing increases in diversity.

AQUITANIAN STAGE

The Aquitanian Stage is the earliest and lowermost division of Miocene rocks, representing all rocks deposited worldwide during the Aquitanian Age (23 million to 20.4 million years ago) of the Neogene Period. The stage is named for exposures in the region of Aquitaine in southwestern France.

The Global Stratotype Section and Point (GSSP) defining the lower boundary of this stage, ratified by the International Commission on Stratigraphy (ICS) in 1996, is located in the Lemme-Carrosio Section within the village of Carrosio, Italy. This lower boundary closely coincides with the base of the zone of the foraminiferan (pseudopod-using unicellular organism protected by a test, or shell) *Paragloborotalia kugleri* and the first occurrence of the calcareous nannofossil (remains of ocean-dwelling golden-brown algae) *Sphenolithus capricornutus*. The Aquitanian Stage underlies the Burdigalian Stage and overlies the Chattian Stage of the Paleogene System.

BURDIGALIAN STAGE

The second of six stages subdividing Miocene rocks, the Burdigalian Stage corresponds to all rocks deposited worldwide during the Burdigalian Age (20.4 million to 16 million years ago) of the Neogene Period. The stage is named for outcrops in the French region of Bordeaux (ancient Burdigala), particularly for the fossiliferous *faluns de Bordeaux* in the Aquitaine Basin of southwestern France. The formal lower boundary of the Burdigalian Stage has yet to be established, but the upper boundary approximates the zone of the first appearance of the foraminiferan (pseudopod-using unicellular organism protected by a test or shell) *Globigerinatella insueta*.

LANGHIAN STAGE

The Langhian Stage is the third of six divisions of Miocene rocks, embodying all rocks deposited worldwide during the Langhian Age (16 million to 13.8 million years ago) of the Neogene Period. The Langhian Stage is named for the region of Langhe, north of the town of Ceva in northern Italy.

The lower boundary of the Langhian Stage has been set near the base of the zone of the foraminiferan (a pseudopod-using unicellular organism protected by a test or shell) *Praeorbulina glomerosa*. The upper boundary has been placed just below the last occurrence of the calcareous nannoplankton (a single-celled, photosynthetic organism with a shell made up of calcium carbonate plates called coccoliths) *Sphenolithus heteromorphus*.

SERRAVALLIAN STAGE

The Serravallian Stage is the fourth division of middle Miocene rocks, representing all rocks deposited worldwide during the Serravallian Age (13.8 million to 11.6 million years ago) of the Neogene Period. The Serravallian Stage is named for outcrops in the vicinity of Serravalle in the Scrivia Valley in Alessandria, Italy.

The lower boundary of the Serravallian Stage nearly matches the extinction level of the calcareous nanno-plankton (a single-celled, photosynthetic organism with a shell made up of calcium carbonate plates called cocco-liths) *Sphenolithus heteromorphus* and the first occurrence of the foraminiferan (pseudopod-using unicellular organism protected by a test, or shell) *Fohsella fohsi*. The upper boundary is nearly coincident with the first appearance of the foraminiferan *Neogloboquadrina acostaensis*.

Tortonian Stage

The Tortonian Stage is the fifth division of Miocene rocks, corresponding to all rocks deposited worldwide during the Tortonian Age (11.6 million to 7.2 million years ago) of the Neogene Period. The stage is named for expo-sures in the region of Tortona, in the Italian Piedmont. The Tortonian and the preceding Serravallian are some-times treated as subdivisions of another stage, the Vindobonian, but they are sufficiently distinct to warrant different names.

The GSSP defining the lower boundary of this stage, ratified by the ICS in 2003, is located in the Monte dei Corvi Beach section approximately 5 km (3 miles) south-east of Ancona, Italy. The lower boundary coincides with the last common occurrence of the calcareous nannofossil (remains of ocean-dwelling golden-brown algae composed of calcite platelets) *Discoaster kugleri* and the foraminiferan (pseudopod-using unicellular organism protected by a test or shell) *Globigerinoides subquadratus*. This upper boundary nearly matches the base of the zones of the foraminiferan

Globorotalia miotumida and calcareous nannofossil *Amaurolithus delicatus*.

MESSINIAN STAGE

The Messinian Stage is the uppermost division of Miocene rocks, encompassing all rocks deposited worldwide during the Messinian Age (7.2 million to 5.3 million years ago) of the Neogene Period. The Messinian Stage is named for marine strata near Messina, Sicily.

The GSSP defining the lower boundary of this stage, ratified by the ICS in 2000, is located in the Oued Akrech near Rabat, Mor. This boundary is nearly coincident with the base of the zone of the foraminiferan *Globorotalia miotumida* and the calcareous nannofossil (remains of ocean-dwelling golden-brown algae composed of calcite platelets) *Amaurolithus delicatus*. The upper boundary of the Messinian coincides with the first appearance of the calcareous nannofossil *Ceratolithus acutus*. The Messinian Stage overlies the Tortonian Stage and underlies the Zanclean Stage.

THE PLIOCENE EPOCH

The Pliocene Epoch is the second of two major worldwide divisions of the Neogene Period, spanning the interval from about 5.3 million to 2.6 million years ago. The Pliocene follows the Miocene Epoch (23 million to 5.3 million years ago) and is further subdivided into two ages and their corresponding rock stages: the Zanclean (5.3 million to 3.6 million years ago) and the Piacenzian (3.6 million to 2.6 million years ago). The Pliocene Epoch precedes the Pleistocene Epoch of the Quaternary Period.

Pliocene terrestrial and marine deposits are known throughout the world. For example, Early Pliocene marine deposits are well known from the Mediterranean region, and Late Pliocene marine deposits can be found in Britain and the Atlantic coastal plain of North America. The Siwalik Range of India and Pakistan and the Henan and Shanxi provinces of China also contain Pliocene terrestrial deposits.

Pliocene environments were generally cooler and drier than those of preceding epochs, as revealed by the remains of plants and trees, but marine records indicate that an interval around 3–3.5 million years ago may have been a relatively warm period, at least in the North Atlantic.

A modern aspect is seen in Pliocene terrestrial vertebrate faunas of the Northern Hemisphere. Older groups of animals became extinct throughout the preceding Miocene Epoch. Although similarities are evident between the faunas of Eurasia and North America, little faunal interchange appears to have occurred between the two regions. The similarities probably result from the continuation of forms that migrated between the two areas late in the Miocene. During the Early Pliocene, a remarkably homogeneous fauna probably existed from Spain and Africa to China. Mastodons (elephant-like animals) underwent a great evolutionary diversification during the Pliocene, and many variant forms developed, adapted to varying ecological environments. In North America, rhinoceroses became extinct. Camels, some of large size, were abundant and diverse, as were horses.

The more advanced primates continued to evolve in the Pliocene, with australopithecines, the first creatures that can be termed human, appearing early in the epoch. A burst of particularly rapid evolutionary change and diversification in primates, as well as other African mammals, appears to have occurred around 2.5 million years ago near the boundary of the Pliocene and Pleistocene, possibly connected to drying associated with the expansion of northern hemisphere glaciers around this time. The land connection between North and South America became reestablished in the mid-Pliocene, around 3.5 million years ago, allowing many terrestrial mammals including ground sloths, glyptodonts (large, armadillo-like, armoured animals), armadillos, opossums, and porcupines to appear in the Late Pliocene fossil record of North America. (Previously, they were isolated on the South American continent.)

Marine faunas (including corals, predatory gastropods, and others) in the Western Atlantic and Caribbean experienced a period of transition during the Late Pliocene, with many forms becoming extinct and others appearing for the first time. These changes have been attributed to variations in both temperature and oceanic nutrient supplies in the region.

ZANCLEAN STAGE

The Zanclean Stage is the lowermost division of Pliocene rocks, encompassing all rocks deposited worldwide during the Zanclean Age (5.3 million to 3.6 million years ago) of the Neogene Period. The Zanclean Stage is named for Zancla, the pre-Roman name for Messina in Sicily.

The Global Stratotype Section and Point (GSSP) defining the lower boundary of this stage, ratified by the International Commission on Stratigraphy (ICS) in 2000, is located in the Eraclea Minoa section on the southern coast of Sicily. The lower boundary of the Zanclean Stage is nearly coincident with the first occurrence of *Ceratolithus actus* and the last occurrence of *Discoaster quinqueramus*. Both species are calcareous nannoplankton (single-celled, photosynthetic organisms with shells made up of calcium carbonate plates called coccoliths). The upper boundary occurs just above the extinction margin of the foraminiferan (pseudopod-using unicellular organism protected by a test, or shell) *Globorotalia margaritae*. The Zanclean Stage underlies the Piacenzian Stage and follows the Messinian Stage.

PIACENZIAN STAGE

The Piacenzian Stage, the uppermost division of Pliocene rocks, represents all rocks deposited worldwide during the Piacenzian Age (3.6 million to 2.6 million years ago) of the Neogene Period (the past 23 million years). The Piacenzian Stage is named for the city of Piacenza, which lies midway between Parma and Milan in Italy.

The GSSP defining the lower boundary of this stage, ratified by the ICS in 1997, is located on Punta Piccola near Porto Empedocle along the southern coast of Sicily. This lower boundary coincides with the first appearance of the foraminiferan (pseudopod-using unicellular organism protected by a test, or shell) *Globorotalia crassaformis* in Mediterranean regions and the extinction levels of the foraminiferans *G. margaritae* and *Pulleniatina primalis* in low and middle latitudes outside the Mediterranean. The upper boundary coincides with the extinction levels of the calcareous nannofossils (remains of ocean-dwelling golden-brown algae composed of calcite platelets) *Discoaster pentaradiatus* and *D. surculus*. The Piacenzian Stage overlies the Zanclean Stage and underlies the Gelasian Stage, the first stage of the Pleistocene Epoch in the Quaternary Period.

SIGNIFICANT LIFE-FORMS OF THE NEOGENE PERIOD

Neogene mammals had more in common with their counterparts from modern times. For example, cave bears and members of the genus *Camelops* bore striking similarities to modern bears and camels, respectively. In addition, the fossils of several apes and other primates, such as *Dryopithecus*, *Gigantopithecus*, and *Ramapithecus*, also date to Neogene times and were useful for increasing the understanding of human origins.

CAMELOPS

Camelops is an extinct genus of large camels that existed from the Late Pliocene Epoch to the end of the Pleistocene Epoch (between 3.6 million and 11,700 years ago) in western North America from Mexico to Alaska. *Camelops* is unknown east of the Mississippi River.

Six species are currently recognized, but the taxonomy of this genus is in need of revision. A true camel, it resembled the slightly smaller existent Arabian camel (*Camelus dromedarius*) in structure. It had long robust legs and a long neck, and it probably had a single hump because it has elongated spines only on the vertebrae over its anterior back.

Camelops became extinct in North America near the close of the Pleistocene, as did many large mammals. The cause of this large-scale extinction is unknown.

CAVE BEAR

The cave bear (*Ursus spelaeus*) is an extinct species of bear, notable for its habit of inhabiting caves, where its remains are frequently preserved. The remains of more than 100,000 cave bears have been found in European cave deposits. The cave bear is best known from late Pleistocene cave deposits, but it can be traced back to Late Pliocene times (the Pliocene Epoch ended about 2.6 million years ago and was followed by the Pleistocene). Remains have been found in England, Belgium, Germany, Russia, Spain, Italy, and Greece, and it may have reached North Africa. Several local varieties, or races, have been described, including dwarf races from some regions. Stone Age peoples sometimes hunted the cave bear, but evidence of this hunting is so sporadic that it is highly unlikely that hunting by man caused its extinction. It appears likely that most cave bears died in the severe glacial winters during hibernation. The remains include a large proportion of particularly young or old and many specimens showing unmistakable signs of illness or disease. Extinction of the cave bear seems to have been a gradual process that was complete at the close of the last glacial episode. The cave bear was probably as large as the Kodiak bears of Alaska, the largest bears of today. The head was very large, and the jaws bore distinctive teeth. It has been inferred that the animal was largely vegetarian.

CHALICOTHERIUM

Chalicotherium is a genus of extinct perissodactyls, the order including the horse and rhinoceros. Fossil remains of the genus are common in deposits of Asia, Europe, and Africa from the Miocene Epoch (23 million to 5.3 million years ago). The genus persisted into the following Pliocene Epoch, and remains of a related genus, *Moropus,* are found in North America.

European cave bear (Ursus spelaeus). Courtesy of the American Museum of Natural History, New York

Chalicotherium and its relatives, collectively known as the chalicotheres, were quite unusual in appearance and structure. In overall appearance the body and slim skull were horselike.

The teeth were distinctive in structure and unhorselike. The front limbs were longer than the hind limbs, and the back sloped downward. The feet were quite distinctive. Rather than hooves, each of the three toes on each foot terminated in a strongly developed claw. It is probable that the development of claws was related to the feeding habits of the animal. *Chalicotherium* may have browsed on branches of trees, pulling them down with the front claws. The claws may also have been employed to dig up roots and tubers.

DINOHYUS

Dinohyus is an extinct genus of giant piglike mammals found as fossils in deposits of early Miocene age in North America. *Dinohyus* is the last and largest of a group of mammals called entelodonts, an early offshoot of the primitive swine stock. As large as a bison, it stood at least 2 metres (6 feet) tall at the shoulder. The skull alone was about 1 metre (more than 3 feet) long and had many bony flanges and protuberances, but the braincase was extremely small. The teeth were distinctive: the incisors were blunt, while the canines were stout and must have been effective weapons. *Dinohyus* was probably a root eater. The neck was short and thick, and the spines in the anterior elements of the backbone were rather long and formed a pronounced hump at the shoulders of the animal.

DRYOPITHECUS

Dryopithecus is a genus of extinct ape that is representative of early members of the lineage that includes humans and other apes. Although *Dryopithecus* has been known by a variety of names based upon fragmentary material found over a widespread area including Europe, Africa, and Asia,

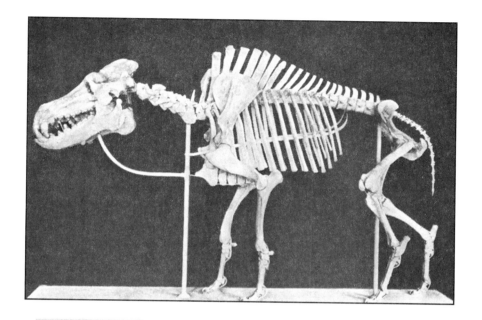

Dinohyus hollandi *skeleton.* Courtesy of the American Museum of Natural History, New York

it appears probable that only a single genus is represented. *Dryopithecus* is found as fossils in Miocene and Pliocene deposits (23 million to 2.6 million years old) and apparently originated in Africa.

Several distinct forms of *Dryopithecus* are known, including small, medium, and large, gorilla-sized animals. In many ways, as might be expected, *Dryopithecus* is rather generalized in structure and lacks most of the specializations that distinguish living humans and other living apes. The canine teeth are larger than those in humans but not as strongly developed as those in other living apes. The limbs were not excessively long. The skull lacked the well-developed crests and massive brow ridges found in modern apes.

Dryopithecus was a distant Miocene forerunner of gorillas and chimpanzees. A form close to this branching of the dryopithecine stock is represented by the genus *Ramapithecus,* distinguished by its more advanced dentition. The dryopithecines probably inhabited forested areas.

GIGANTOPITHECUS

Gigantopithecus is a genus of large fossil ape, of which two species are known: *G. bilaspurensis*, which lived 6 to 9 million years ago in India, and *G. blacki*, which lived in China until at least 1 million years ago. These apes are known from teeth, lower jaw bones, and possibly a piece of distal humerus. They may have been larger than gorillas. *Gigantopithecus* lived in open country and had powerful grinding and chewing teeth.

The first specimens were found by the German-Dutch paleontologist G.H.R. von Koenigswald in Chinese drugstores, where they were known as "dragon's teeth." The teeth, though large, have a few similarities to human teeth, and this led some paleomorphologists to speculate that humans might have had "giant" ancestors. Later discoveries of complete jaw bones demonstrated that they were from extinct apes.

GLANS

Glans is a genus of small pelecypods (clams) especially characteristic of the Miocene Epoch. The ornamentation of the shell includes prominent ribbing that extends from the apex to the broadly expanding margin. The ribs are broken up into a nodose pattern by fine lines, perpendicular to their axis of growth. Internally, the margin of the shell has a denticulate pattern formed by alternating ridges and troughs.

Glyptodon

Glyptodon is a genus of extinct giant mammals related to modern armadillos found as fossils in deposits in North and South America dating from the Pliocene and Pleistocene epochs (5.3 million to 11,700 years ago). *Glyptodon* and its close relatives, the glyptodonts, were encased from head to tail in thick, protective armour resembling in shape the shell of a turtle but composed of bony plates much like the covering of an armadillo. The body shell alone was as long as 1.5 metres (5 feet). The tail, also clad in armour, could serve as a lethal club. Indeed, in some relatives of *Glyptodon*, the tip of the tail was a knob of bone that was sometimes spiked. Glyptodonts ate almost anything: plants, carrion, or insects.

Mastodon

Mastodon is a name that refers to any of several extinct elephantine mammals (family Mastodontidae, genus *Mastodon* [also called *Mammut*]) that first appeared in the early Miocene and continued in various forms through the Pleistocene Epoch. In North America, mastodons probably persisted into post-Pleistocene time and were thus

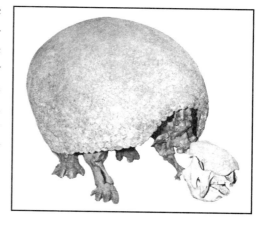

Glyptodont (genus Glyptodon). Courtesy of the trustees of the British Museum (Natural History); photograph, Imitor

American mastodon woolly mammoth African savanna elephant

Mastodons and woolly mammoths were hunted by some Paleo-Indians. These animals were similar in size to modern African elephants but, unlike the modern variety, they were adapted to ice age temperatures. Encyclopædia Britannica, Inc.

contemporaneous with historic North American Indian groups. Mastodons had a worldwide distribution because their remains are quite common and are often particularly well preserved.

A characteristic feature of the mastodons, which appear to have fed on leaves, is the distinctive nature of the grinding teeth, which in many respects are relatively primitive. They are low-crowned, large, and strongly rooted, with as many as four prominent ridges separated by deep troughs. The teeth are much smaller and less complex, however, than those in the true elephants. The prominent upper tusks were long and grew parallel to each other with an upward curvature. Short lower tusks were present in males but absent in females.

Mastodons were shorter than modern elephants but were heavily built. Although the skull was lower and flatter and of generally simpler construction than that of the modern elephants, it was similar in appearance. The ears were smaller and not as prominent as those of elephants. The body was relatively long, and the legs were short, massive, and pillarlike. Mastodons were covered with long, reddish brown hair. The reasons for their extinction are uncertain, but, in North America at least, human hunting may have played a role.

MERYCHIPPUS

Merychippus is an extinct genus of early horses, found as fossils in deposits from the Middle and Late Miocene Epoch (16.4 million to 5.3 million years ago). *Merychippus* descended from the earlier genus *Parahippus*.

The tooth pattern in *Merychippus* is basically the same as that in the modern horse. The teeth became higher and dental cement appeared, which allowed a grazing mode of life. Other developments in the skeleton are also evident: its size increased so that *Merychippus* was almost as large as a modern pony, and the skull became more elongated in an especially horselike fashion. The limbs also became more horselike in proportion and better adapted to running. In some forms the three toes remained comparatively large, but in progressive species of *Merychippus* the two side toes were short and small. The centre toe was much larger than the others and carried most of the animal's weight. A well-developed hoof was present on the large central toe.

MOROPUS

An extinct genus of the chalicotheres, *Moropus* is the name of a group of unusual perissodactyls ("odd-toed" ungulates) related to the horse. Fossil remains of *Moropus* are found in Miocene deposits in North America and Asia. *Moropus* was as large as a modern horse, but, unlike other perissodactyls, it had claws instead of hoofs. The forelimbs were longer than the hind limbs, and the back sloped downward to the hindquarters. The teeth possessed low crowns; the molars were large and the premolars small. It is likely that *Moropus* did not browse or graze as did other horselike forms but instead probably used its large claws to dig up roots and tubers more suited to its type of dentition than grasses.

OREOPITHECUS

An extinct genus of primates found as fossils in Late Miocene deposits in East Africa and Early Pliocene deposits in southern Europe (11.6 million to 3.6 million years ago), *Oreopithecus* is best known from complete but crushed specimens found in coal deposits in Europe. The relation of the genus to other primates has been a matter of some debate and confusion. *Oreopithecus* appears to combine primitive and advanced features that, on one hand, seem to ally it with the Old World monkeys and, on the other, with the advanced, manlike apes. It is probable that *Oreopithecus* represents a specialized side branch of primate evolution that did not give rise to more advanced forms; it is generally included in a separate ape family, the Oreopithecidae.

Oreopithecus, an inhabitant of swampy regions, was about 1.2 metres (4 feet) tall and had long arms. It is estimated that *Oreopithecus* weighed about 40 kg (90 pounds). The skull was small and the teeth were specialized, so it probably ate soft plant foods. It is doubtful that *Oreopithecus* habitually stood erect.

PLIOHIPPUS

Pliohippus is an extinct genus of horses that inhabited North America during the Pliocene Epoch (5.3–2.6 million years ago). *Pliohippus*, the earliest one-toed horse, evolved from *Merychippus*, a three-toed horse of the preceding Miocene Epoch. The teeth of *Pliohippus* are taller and more complexly folded than those of earlier horses, indicating a greater dependence on grazing than browsing for food. Because of its diet and its specializations for running, it is likely that *Pliohippus* lived on open plains.

RAMAPITHECUS

Ramapithecus is a fossil primate genus that dates from the Middle and Late Miocene epochs (about 16.6 million to 5.3 million years ago). For a time in the 1960s and '70s, *Ramapithecus* was thought to be the first direct ancestor of modern humans.

The first *Ramapithecus* fossils (fragments of an upper jaw and some teeth) were discovered in 1932 in fossil deposits in the Siwālik hills of northern India. No significance was attached to these fossils until 1960, when Elwyn Simons of Yale University began studying them and fit the jaw fragments together. Based on his observations of the shape of the jaw and of the dentition, which he thought were transitional between those of apes and humans, Simons advanced the theory that *Ramapithecus* represented the first step in the evolutionary divergence of humans from the common hominoid stock that produced modern apes and humans.

Simons's theory was strongly supported by his student David Pilbeam, and it soon gained wide acceptance among anthropologists. The age of the fossils (about 14 million years) fit well with the then-prevailing notion that the ape-human split had occurred at least 15 million years ago. The first challenge to the theory came in the late 1960s from biochemist Allan Wilson and anthropologist Vincent Sarich, who, at the University of California at Berkeley, had been comparing the molecular chemistry of albumins (blood proteins) among various animal species. They concluded that the ape-human divergence must have occurred much later than the dates for *Ramapithecus*. (It is now thought that the final split took place some 6 to 8 million years ago.)

Wilson and Sarich's argument was initially dismissed by anthropologists, but biochemical and fossil evidence mounted in favour of it. Finally, in 1976 Pilbeam discovered a complete *Ramapithecus* jaw, not far from the initial fossil find, that had a distinctive V shape and thus differed markedly from the parabolic shape of hominid jaws. He soon repudiated his belief in *Ramapithecus* as a human ancestor, and the theory was largely abandoned by the early 1980s. *Ramapithecus* fossils subsequently were found to resemble those of the fossil primate genus *Sivapithecus* (*q.v.*), which is now regarded as ancestral to the orangutan. Support also increased for the theory that *Ramapithecus* probably should be included in the *Sivapithecus* genus.

RIVERSLEIGH FOSSILS

These are any of numerous assemblages of fossils found at Riversleigh Station, in northwestern Queensland, Australia, which together constitute the richest and most diverse collection of fossils ever found on that continent. Riversleigh is an isolated area about 140 miles (225 km) northwest of the city of Mount Isa. The fossils are found in limestone rock outcrops near the Gregory River. Since the Australian paleontologist Michael Archer began intensive explorations of the area in 1983, Riversleigh has yielded the remains of more than 200 previously unknown species of vertebrates. Most specimens lived in the Miocene Epoch or in the succeeding Pliocene Epoch. The finds included many types of early (and extinct) marsupials, ranging from a large carnivorous kangaroo and marsupial "lions" and "wolves" to miniature koalas and phalangers.

Other finds included dozens of new species of bats, a pre-historic type of platypus, and several unknown species of reptiles and rodents. The Riversleigh fossils vastly expanded existing knowledge of Australia's prehistoric life and of the evolutionary history of its marsupials.

SIVAPITHECUS

Sivapithecus is a fossil primate genus that dates from the Miocene Epoch and thought to be the direct ancestor of the orangutan. *Sivapithecus* is closely related to *Ramapithecus,* and fossils of the two primates have often been recovered from the same deposits in the Siwālik Hills of northern Pakistan. Other *Sivapithecus* remains have been found at sites in Turkey, Pakistan, China, Greece, and Kenya. Some authorities maintain that *Sivapithecus* and *Ramapithecus* are in fact the same species. Although *Sivapithecus* was slightly larger than *Ramapithecus,* it was only a small-to-medium-sized ape about the size of a modern chimpanzee. The fossil remains of *Sivapithecus* reveal that it shared many of the same specialized facial features of the orangutan—eyes set narrowly apart, a con-cave face, a smooth nasal floor, large zygomatic bones, and enlarged central incisors.

Sivapithecus' place in primate evolution was poorly understood until the 1980s. Previously, the genus, along with *Ramapithecus,* was interpreted as having both apelike and humanlike features and thus was presumed to be a possible first step in the evolutionary divergence of humans from the common hominoid stock of the apes. But new *Sivapithecus* finds and the reinterpretation of existing remains convinced most authorities in the 1980s that *Sivapithecus* was the ancestor of the modern orang-utan and diverged from the common lineage of the African apes (that is, chimpanzees and gorillas) and humans more than 13 million years ago. The earliest *Sivapithecus* remains found so far are about 17 million years old, and the most recent are about 8 million years old.

THYLACOSMILUS

Thylacosmilus is an extinct genus of carnivorous marsupials found as fossils in deposits dated from about 10 million to 3 million years ago (late Miocene to late Pliocene Epoch) in South America. *Thylacosmilus* was sabre-toothed and about as large as a modern jaguar (*Panthera onca*). To a remarkable degree, *Thylacosmilus* paralleled the evolution of sabre-toothed cats. Its canine teeth were long and powerfully developed for stabbing prey and fit into a well-developed flange, or projecting edge, in the chin region of the lower jaw. *Thylacosmilus* became extinct after the land connection between North and South America was established during the middle of the Pliocene Epoch.

CHAPTER 5

THE QUATERNARY PERIOD

In the geologic history of Earth, the Quaternary Period is a unit of time within the Cenozoic Era, beginning 2,588,000 years ago and continuing to the present day. The Quaternary has been characterized by several periods of glaciation (the "ice ages" of common lore), when ice sheets many kilometres thick have covered vast areas of the continents in temperate areas. During and between these glacial periods, rapid changes in climate and sea level have occurred, and environments worldwide have been altered. These variations in turn have driven rapid changes in life-forms, both flora and fauna. Beginning some 200,000 years ago, they were responsible for the rise of modern humans.

The Quaternary is one of the best-studied parts of the geologic record. In part this is because it is well preserved in comparison with the other periods of geologic time. Less of it has been lost to erosion, and the sediments are not usually altered by rock-forming processes. Quaternary rocks and sediments, being the most recently laid geologic strata, can be found at or near the surface of the Earth in valleys and on plains, seashores, and even the seafloor. These deposits are important for unraveling geologic history because they are most easily compared to modern sedimentary deposits. The environments and geologic processes earlier in the period were similar to those of today; a large proportion of Quaternary fossils are related to living organisms; and numerous dating techniques can be used to provide relatively precise timing of events and rates of change.

The term Quaternary originated early in the 19th century when it was applied to the youngest deposits in the Paris Basin in France by French geologist Jules Desnoyers, who followed an antiquated method of referring to geologic eras as "Primary," "Secondary," "Tertiary," and so on. Beginning with the work of Scottish geologist Charles Lyell in the 1830s, the Quaternary Period was divided into two epochs, the Pleistocene and the Holocene, with the Pleistocene (and therefore the Quaternary) understood to have begun some 1.8 million years ago. In 1948 a decision was made at the 18th International Geological Congress (IGC) in London that the base of the Pleistocene Series should be fixed in marine rocks exposed in the coastal areas of Calabria in southern Italy. As ratified by the International Commission on Stratigraphy (ICS) in 1985, the type section for boundary between the Pleistocene and the earlier Pliocene occurs in a sequence of 1.8-million-year-old marine strata at Vrica in Calabria. However, no decision was made to equate the beginning of the Pleistocene Epoch to the beginning of the Quaternary Period, and indeed the very status of the Quaternary as a period within the geologic time scale had come into question. Various gatherings of the IGC in the 19th and 20th centuries had agreed to retain both the Tertiary and Quaternary as useful time units, particularly for climatic- and continent-based studies, but a growing number of geologists came to favour dividing the Cenozoic Era into two other periods, the Paleogene and the Neogene. In 2005 the ICS decided to recommend keeping the Tertiary and Quaternary in the time scale, but only as informal sub-eras of the Cenozoic.

The ICS abandoned the sub-era structure in 2008, deciding instead to formally designate the Quaternary as the uppermost period of the Cenozoic Era, following the aforementioned Paleogene and Neogene periods. In 2009 the International Union of Geological Sciences (IUGS) officially ratified the decision to set the beginning of the Quaternary at 2,588,000 years ago, a time when rock strata show extensive evidence of widespread expansion of ice sheets over the northern continents and the beginning of an era of dramatic climatic and oceanographic change. This time is coincident with the beginning of the Gelasian Age, which was officially designated by the IUGS and the ICS in 2009 as the lowermost stage of the Pleistocene Epoch. The type section for the Gelasian Stage, the rock layer laid down during the Gelasian Age, is found at Monte San Nicola near Gela, Sicily.

THE QUATERNARY ENVIRONMENT

Glaciation sets the Quaternary Period apart from the other periods of the Cenozoic. This phenomenon transformed many near-polar and temperate regions through climatic disruption and the sheer weight of ice on the land. The conversion of large amounts of liquid water into ice lowered global sea levels, which created vast land bridges, such as those connecting Alaska to Siberia and Australia to Southeast Asia.

GLACIATION

The most distinctive changes seen during the Quaternary were the advances of ice into temperate latitudes of the Northern Hemisphere. The glacial landscapes were dominated by ice several kilometres thick that covered all but the highest peaks in the interior. Grounded ice extended onto the continental shelf in the Barents, Kara, and Laptev seas, much of the Canadian coast, and the Gulf of Maine.

Ice shelves similar to those seen today in the Ross and Weddell seas of Antarctica are postulated to have existed in the Norwegian Sea and the Gulf of Maine and were likely in many other settings. High ice and domes of cold high-pressure air displaced the polar jet streams, steering storm tracks south to the glacial margins and beyond. In addition, cold sinking air over the ice sheets created strong down-flowing katabatic winds, drying land near the glaciers. Land close to the glaciers and affected by the cold temperatures (periglacial landscapes) were areas of permafrost and tundra. Farther away, vast dry, cold grasslands (steppes) were formed.

THE "ICE AGES"

It is common to see the "ice age" described in popular magazines as a time in which the "ice caps expanded from the North and South poles to cover much of the Earth." Such descriptions are misleading. In fact, expansion of the Antarctic ice sheets was limited to the Ross and Weddell seas and other shelves, with inland buildup of only a few hundred metres. In the Northern Hemisphere, vast areas that are now ice-free were indeed covered with ice, but the expansion was not from the North Pole. Rather, it spread from the centres of Canada, Scotland, Sweden, and possibly northern Russia. Ice sheets may have pushed out onto continental shelves and formed ice shelves, but in general deep-ocean basins such as the Arctic Ocean were not the centres of growth.

Continental ice sheets formed and extended into temperate latitudes numerous times in the Quaternary, but the terrestrial record of these events is somewhat incomplete. The traditional view is that of only four major glacial periods, or "ice ages." They have been correlated to one another in a rather simple manner and are reflected in the names of some geologic units. However, since the 1950s the marine record has become more useful because of its greater continuity and preservation. Marine cores may contain microscopic fossils of single-celled organisms called foraminifera, whose shells contain a record of water temperature and composition as stable isotopes of oxygen and carbon. These isotopes have revealed that dozens of major glacial-interglacial episodes have taken place during the Quaternary. Even more detailed records have been recovered from cores through glacial ice. On land, the terms *glacial* or *glaciation* describe cold periods of the greatest duration, whereas the intervening warm periods are called interglacials. Shorter glacial episodes are known as stadials, with the corresponding warm intervals being interstadials. Conversely, the marine record uses numbers to designate periods of warming and cooling. Cool stages have even numbers, warm have odd, and the numbers go up as one proceeds from the most recent event to the most distant. The marine stages roughly correspond in length to the stadials and interstadials. Thus, marine isotope Stage 2 was the peak glacial period 11,500–20,000 years ago, while Stage 5 was the peak warm period 70,000–130,000 years ago.

There are four named major glaciations in North America. The earliest, the Nebraskan, is found on the plains of the central United States. The Kansan overlies it and extends slightly farther southwest into Kansas. The Illinoian, as the name implies, terminates primarily in Illinois. The Wisconsin Glacial Stage was extensive in Wisconsin as well as in New York, New England, and the Canadian Maritime Provinces. This last advance removed most evidence of earlier glaciations in these regions. The actual positions of the southern edges of these ice sheets varied considerably from glacial to glacial. The northern extent of the ice is poorly known at best. Similar sequences are found from Scandinavian ice sheets and from ice in the Swiss and Austrian Alps.

GLACIAL REMNANTS

As the ice sheets and smaller glaciers advanced and retreated over Quaternary landscapes, they scoured rocks and soil from the land. This material was transported and deposited to the periphery of the ice sheets in large moraines of glacial till. Meltwater and large blocks of ice left behind from retreating glaciers and ice sheets later formed the glacial lakes that are common in temperate North America and Eurasia and in many alpine regions throughout the world.

Landforms

There have certainly been previous periods of geologic time in which glaciers were extensive (during the late Precambrian and the Permian Period, for example), but the Quaternary has left a distinctive imprint on modern landscapes and surface environments. The most distinguishing characteristics of the Quaternary in middle and high latitudes are glacial sediments and evidence of glacial erosion.

Glacial erosion is the predominant feature of high mountains such as the Alps, Himalayas, Andes, and Rockies. Glacial erosion has sculpted deep alpine valleys, and it has left sharp erosional remnants such as the Matterhorn in Europe. Valley glaciers near the ocean sculpted deep fjords in Norway, Greenland, northern Canada, Alaska, Chile, and Antarctica. Submerged on the continental shelf are even larger sculpted troughs formed by ice streams, large fast-moving tongues of ice draining from continental ice sheets. These troughs are ubiquitous on the Antarctic shelf near the largest modern ice sheet.

Relict examples are found in the Laurentian Trough, the Hudson Strait, the Barents Sea north of Norway, and many other locations. Other large-scale examples of glacial erosion include the Great Lakes and the Finger Lakes of New York. In innumerable smaller examples, a combination of glacial erosion and deposition so altered the landscape as to derange the drainage completely, resulting in the tens of thousands of lakes of Minnesota, Maine, and Alaska as well as Canada, Scandinavia, and northern Russia. Limited examples exist in the Southern Hemisphere, such as the lake districts of New Zealand and Chile.

Glaciers deposit sediments and other geologic debris called till, especially near their bases, sides, or fronts.

This drumlin in Yorkshire, Eng., was formed by glaciers that approached the steep stoss end (right) *and moved along the gently sloping lee end* (left). © Ken Gardner/Landform Slides

Ridges of till and outwash sand left at the terminal or lateral margins of glaciers are known as moraines, and major moraine belts mark former continental ice sheets in the middle portions of North America, Europe, and Scandinavia. Nowhere is the importance of moraines to forming the landscape more evident than Long Island, New York. The entire island is framed by two major terminal moraines (the Harbor Hill and Ronkonkama Moraines) associated with the Laurentide Ice Sheet. First deposited between 22,000 and 18,000 years ago, these glacial sediments were subsequently reworked by coastal and stream processes into the sandy barrier islands off of Long Island's south shore. Other types of glacial deposits are widespread in the Northern Hemisphere north of roughly 40–50° N latitude, forming many landscapes and shorelines.

Till also forms drumlins, streamlined hills that align with former ice movement. Excellent examples are seen in Boston Harbor, Nova Scotia, Ireland, Scandinavia, and northwestern Canada. In other areas, till is more irregular or deposited as a thin blanket over bedrock. Moving water also plays a large part in sediment deposition and subglacial erosion. One of the most striking landforms in formerly glaciated terrain is the esker. Eskers are sinuous ridges 20 or 30 metres (65 or 100 feet) high and hundreds of kilometres in length, with steep side walls. They were deposited in pressurized tunnels at the base of ice sheets during melting phases. They are well displayed in Ontario, Maine, and Sweden. Other ice-contact stratified drift was emplaced adjacent to melting ice walls in valleys (kame terraces), as wet alluvial fans (valley train deposits), and as deltas built into glacial lakes and the sea. Glacial-marine deltas are well exposed in Maine and the Canadian Maritime Provinces, where they provide clear evidence of postglacial sea-level changes—including some terrain that

An esker, a narrow ridge of gravel and sand left by a retreating glacier, winds through western Nunavut, Canada, near the Thelon River. © Richard Alexander Cooke III

has risen more than 100 metres (328 feet) since the ice retreated, a phenomenon called isostatic rebound.

In drier areas extensive sand dunes and loess sheets were produced. Loess blown from outwash fans and river valleys in front of the glaciers accumulated to more than 8 metres (25 feet) in thickness along much of the Mississippi River valley. These deposits become thinner to the east, showing the influence of prevailing westerly winds. Other thick loess deposits are found in Europe and Asia, including extensive sections along the Huang He (Yellow River) west of Beijing.

Lakes

Extensive glacial lakes were formed by a variety of glacial-age dams. They could form simply as pools in the depressions created by the ice sheets, in eroded scours, such as the Great Lakes and the Finger Lakes of New York, by ice dams, or by dams of glacial sediments. Glacial lakes of various sizes ringed the decaying Laurentide Ice Sheet in North America, such as Canada's former Lake Agassiz, leaving extensive laminated silts and clays. Remnants of glacial lakes are found in the great arc of Canadian lakes such as Great Bear, Great Slave, Athabasca, Winnipeg, and the Great Lakes. Similar deposits and remnant lakes are found in Europe and Asia, with evidence that glacial-age rivers may have flowed extensively to the south into the Aral, Caspian, and Black seas.

Away from the direct influence of glaciers, there were also many large pluvial lakes, water bodies formed by heavier rains brought by shifting jet streams and storm tracks. These regions are now dry, including many valleys in Nevada and Utah that now contain dry salt flats or shrunken remnants. Lake Lahontan and Lake Bonneville were two of the largest of these. The Great Salt Lake is the modern remnant of Lake Bonneville, whose highest shoreline was formed 18,000 years ago, 330 metres (1,000 feet) above the present lake level. Pluvial lakes were formed as far south as Mexico, Africa, and other locations. The timing of their formation, however, does not correlate easily because of the complex patterns of shifting climates. Lakes contain excellent records of climate change in their shorelines, deep-basin sediments, and fossil record. For example, Lake Tulane in Florida has been extensively studied for its fossil pollen, returning a 50,000-year record that seems to correlate with the marine record of Heinrich Events.

SEA-LEVEL CHANGES

Since the early 1970s, the major tool for understanding changes in global ice volumes, temperatures, and sea level has been the record of stable isotopes of oxygen extracted from marine fossils, cave limestone, and ice cores. Oxygen naturally occurs in three isotopes: ^{16}O (99.763 percent), ^{17}O (0.0375 percent), and ^{18}O (0.1995 percent). Oxygen is found in all organisms and many minerals, including the aragonite and calcite that make up the shells of marine microfossils such as foraminifera. Oxygen isotopes are useful for geologic studies because of the temperature-dependent rate of uptake of the different isotopes by marine organisms. Also, the isotopic composition of seawater is changed by evaporation and precipitation. For example, because it is heavier, ^{18}O is less likely to evaporate. Thus, the vapour will become "lighter," being enriched with ^{16}O, while the remaining seawater will become slightly "heavier," as it is enriched in ^{18}O. During glacial periods, the "light" ice is sequestered on land in glaciers, while ^{18}O concentrates in the oceans. Also, in glacial stages foraminifera form their shells in equilibrium with the ambient water, so the oxygen isotope ratio in foraminifera shells is directly representative of the global volume of glacial ice. This in turn can be read as a record of sea-level change, because the water required to make the major ice sheets comes ultimately from the ocean. However, the isotope record must be calibrated to independent information from dated marine shorelines.

The record of ice-volume changes in oxygen isotopes, calibrated to sites on oceanic islands, implies that at the peak of the most recent glacial stage 18,000 calendar years ago, sea level was some 120 metres (390 feet) lower than today's. Today's continental shelves and offshore banks were exposed, and there was about 18 percent more land than there is today, taking up an area equal to that of Europe and South America combined. During deglaciation, especially for the period of rapid change between 14,000 and 6,000 years ago, continuous input of glacial meltwater and occasional rapid pulses caused flooding of the lowlands that are now the continental shelves. River valleys became estuaries, such as Chesapeake Bay of North America, the Río de la Plata of South America, and the Gironde Estuary of France, whereas some were inundated to remain as low channels on the continental shelf, such as the Hudson Shelf Valley off of New York City.

Some continental shelves formed land bridges between landmasses that are now separate islands or continents. The most important of these connected Asia and North America at what is now the Bering Strait. Similar land bridges in Southeast Asia linked or at least narrowed the waterways between Indonesia, New Guinea, and Australia. Britain was continuous with continental Europe where the English Channel is today. Such land bridges allowed migration of animals and plants during the lowstands, but in high latitudes the effects of cold climate and direct blockage by glaciers could modify their effectiveness. A long-held theory is that human migration into the Western

Hemisphere was delayed until 13,000 years ago, when a favourable arrangement of Beringia (the land bridge across the Bering Sea) and an ice-free corridor through Alaska formed. More recent studies suggest that the first human migrations into the New World may have been earlier and via other routes, including by boat, but Beringia was undoubtedly the highway for many Pleistocene animals and plants that crossed between the Americas and Asia.

Future sea-level changes have been predicted by the Intergovernmental Panel on Climate Change. These are based on computer models of global warming caused by increased amounts of greenhouse gases in the Earth's atmosphere. The models predict that sea level could rise from 30 to 100 cm (12 to 39 inches) in the next century, disturbing many if not all coastal communities. Of even greater concern, some of the world's major glaciers are marine-based, that is, grounded on land below sea level. A change in sea level and climate could cause the West Antarctic Ice Sheet to surge into the sea in a matter of centuries. If melted (or floated), West Antarctic ice would cause a rise of more than 6 metres (20 feet) of sea level worldwide, flooding major cities such as Miami, New Orleans, London, Venice, and Shanghai. The Greenland Ice Sheet contains about the same volume, whereas the East Antarctic Ice Sheet contains enough water to raise sea level about 60 metres (200 feet). It appears, however, that both the Greenland and East Antarctic ice sheets are inherently more stable than the West Antarctic Ice Sheet.

PALEOCLIMATE

The best records of climate change during the Quaternary are oxygen isotope records taken from deep-sea cores and glacial ice cores. These records are representative of changes in ice volume and temperature, and they reflect global processes as well as some local conditions. They provide measures of the magnitude of changes and the timing of cycles, which can then be related to sedimentary sequences on land and ocean margins. Cycles of humidity and dryness can be determined from lake levels, pollen records, dust in ice cores, and computer modeling.

Oxygen isotope records indicate that, during peak glacial levels of the Quaternary, the Greenland summit was more than 20°C (36°F) colder than present. Vostok Station, Antarctica, may have declined by 15°C (27°F) from its already frigid mean annual temperature of -55°C (-67°F). Similar extremes are assumed to have occurred on and near the major Pleistocene ice sheets. From the records of pollen and plant fossils, reconstructions of the last glacial termination in northern Europe, Scandinavia, and North America show July temperatures 10–15°C (18–27°F) less than present, as well as similar ranges for mean annual temperature. Reconstructions of changes in the tropics have been more controversial. Marine microfossils have been interpreted as indicating temperatures only 1–2°C (2–4°F) cooler than the present, whereas ice cores from a mountain glacier in the tropical Andes imply cooling of 5–8°C (9–14°F), the latter range in accordance with strontium-calcium ratios in fossil corals. Recent techniques of chemical analysis of deep sea sediments suggest a cooling of 2–3°C (4–5°F) at the surface of the tropical Pacific. These differences may seem to be small, but they have important implications for understanding the processes of ocean and atmospheric circulation.

QUATERNARY LIFE

The length of the Quaternary is short relative to geologic and evolutionary time scales, but the rate of evolutionary change during this period is high. It is a basic tenet of ecology that disturbance increases diversity and ultimately leads to evolutionary pressures. The Quaternary is replete with forces of disturbance and evidence for evolution in many living systems. Examples of disturbance include the direct destruction of habitat by glacial advance, the drying of vast plains, increases in size of lakes, a decrease in the area of warm, shallow, continental shelves and carbonate banks, and shifts in ocean currents and fronts.

Fauna and Flora

Ninety percent of the animals represented by Quaternary fossils were recognized by Charles Lyell as being similar to modern forms. Many genera and even species of shellfish, insects, marine microfossils, and terrestrial mammals living today are similar or identical to their Pleistocene ancestors. However, many Pleistocene fossils demonstrate spectacular differences. For example, sabre-toothed cats, woolly mammoths, and cave bears are widely known from museum exhibits and popular literature but are extinct today. Expansion of some environments, such as vast dry steppe grasslands, were favourable areas for bison, horses, antelopes, and their predators. Some species with modern relatives, including the woolly mammoth and woolly rhinoceros, were clearly adapted to the cold tundra regions because of their heavy fur. Some, such as the modern musk ox, would have been right at home.

The Pleistocene is generally recognized as a time of gigantism in terrestrial mammals. The causes for such gigantism are not completely understood, but they most likely include a response to colder conditions and an improved ability to resist predators and reach food higher on shrubs or buried beneath snow. Giant Pleistocene mammals include the giant beaver, giant sloth, stag-moose, dire wolf, giant short-faced bear of the New World, and cave bear of the Old World. The woolly mammoth and mastodon are rivaled in size only by modern elephants. Other animals displayed extremes in body architecture, such as the huge canine teeth of sabre-toothed cats. It is suggested that an "arms race" between predators and their prey led to these extreme developments.

Although unusually large animals capture people's imaginations, plant fossils are often the workhorse of Quaternary scientists. Pollen is one of the most important tools of correlation in terrestrial settings, and it is often used to extend knowledge from well-dated sequences to less clear situations. Fossil pollen is particularly useful because it is almost indestructible when trapped in lake and bog sediments. Pollen is representative of local and regional plant communities and is diagnostic of humid versus dry periods and temperature changes. Changing patterns of pollen can thus trace deglaciation and shifts in vegetation zones. Unlike animals, plants do not migrate, but plant assemblages gradually adjust to long-term changes in humidity and temperature. The classic pollen assemblages of northern Europe have long been used to subdivide the latest Pleistocene and Holocene epochs. In southern Scandinavia these zones track abrupt shifts such as the Younger Dryas cooling and the gradual early Holocene change from boreal to warmer climate assemblages. There were alterations in the abundance of various plants during the changes, and many environments typical of deglaciation or the early Holocene would have looked quite different from the groups that occupy relatively similar climate zones today. For example, a fossil site in Pennsylvania dating to about 12,500 years ago records an environment of open land with scattered spruce, pine, and birch trees, bearing some aspects of tundra and some of prairie. No modern counterparts to this mixed environment exist today. Pollen compilations in North America track spruce, oak, pine, maple, and other species in a cinematic series of diagrams showing these changes over the past 18,000 years.

An expansion of dry shortgrass prairie in the rain shadow of the Rocky Mountains may have put tallgrass grazers such as horses and camels at a disadvantage compared with bison. Conversely, expansion of lakes spread many fishes to new sites, some of which are found today in refugia of small ponds that remained as the connected glacial lakes retreated. One extreme example is the spread of the prickly sculpin across the Continental Divide in British Columbia. This fish was able to move from the south and west-flowing Fraser River to the north and east-flowing Parsnip River, apparently as a consequence of ice that temporarily dammed the Fraser.

Evolution in mollusks can be tracked in Pleistocene deposits on the coastal plains of the eastern and southern United States, around the Baltic Sea, and other gently sloping continental margins. It is likely that changing sea levels and shifts of marine regions played a part in the evolutionary pressure. For example, the present U.S. East Coast can be divided at prominent sites such as Cape Hatteras and Georges Bank, where biogeographic regions are controlled by coastal currents, primarily owing to water temperature. At times during the Pleistocene, subtropical conditions extended to the Carolinas and even Virginia. These periods alternated with cooler-than-normal conditions. The rapid shifts in sea level and latitudinal ecosystems created disturbance and mixing of different ecological assemblages, which in turn accelerated evolutionary pressure.

ICE AGE EXTINCTIONS

Ice age extinctions were not democratic. Most animals that became extinct at the end of the Pleistocene were large, and both herbivores and carnivores were affected. This is particularly true in North and South America as well as Australia. Many hypotheses have been proposed for this record, but the "prehistoric overkill hypothesis" blames human hunting for the demise of large animals wherever humans arrived during the past 40,000 to 13,000 years. This concept envisions bands of human hunters sweeping south into the new lands, meeting animals unafraid of these unfamiliar creatures. There are many objections to this theory, including the lack of sufficient linkage between the hunters and the hunted in the archaeological record, the likely small numbers of human hunters, and the survival of bison and other large species. Most important, however, is that the record of decline and extinction in many cases precedes evidence for humans in the New World and Australia. Other likely causes for extinction include loss or change of habitats, direct climatic effects, and changes in the length and intensity of summer and winter conditions. Predators that went extinct in the latest Pleistocene and early Holocene epochs include the dire wolf, American lion, sabre-toothed cat, American cheetah, and short-faced bear. Extinct grazers and browsers include mammoths and mastodons, shrub oxen, woodland musk oxen, camels, llamas, two genera of deer, two genera of pronghorn antelope, stag-moose, and five species of Pleistocene horses. Horses did not return to the New World until shipped across the Atlantic by the Spanish conquistadors.

Hominin Evolution

American paleontologist Elisabeth Vrba and other scientists have suggested that climate changes 2.5 million years ago accelerated the evolution of hominins (members of the human lineage), giving rise to our genus, *Homo*. The details of this process, and the exact pathways of ancestors and descendants, are highly controversial. Even so, most paleoanthropologists and archaeologists believe that a shift from forests to drier savanna lands in Africa imposed evolutionary pressures that favoured an upright stance and ability to run and walk long distances. This posture freed the hands for grasping and made possible the eventual use of tools.

Homo fossils suggest a migration out of Africa to China and Java as early as 1.8 million years ago near the start of the Pleistocene. This "Out of Africa" theory is now interpreted as multiple events over many millennia. *Homo erectus* was well established in eastern and southeastern Asia by 1 million years ago, and another distinctive human precursor (*Homo antecessor*) arrived in Atapuerca, Spain, by 800,000 years ago. A human ancestor named *Homo heidelbergensis* is found from sites in Africa, Europe, and possibly Asia. These fossils date to between 600,000 and 200,000 years ago.

There is no more controversial subject in this field than the identity and fate of the next major group, the Neanderthals (*Homo neanderthalensis*), which flourished between 200,000 and 30,000 years ago in Europe and western Asia. Most recent work suggests that Neanderthals were not the direct ancestors of modern humans, but interbreeding cannot be disproven. Both *Homo neanderthalensis* and our own species, *Homo sapiens*, may have evolved from *H. heidelbergensis*.

Modern humans (*Homo sapiens*) first appeared in Africa about 200,000 to 150,000 years ago. They arrived in the Middle East about 100,000 years ago, apparently living in the same environmental settings as the Neanderthals. Not until 40,000 years ago did modern humans arrive in Europe, but in less than 10,000 years they supplanted Neanderthals completely. *Homo sapiens* also spread into

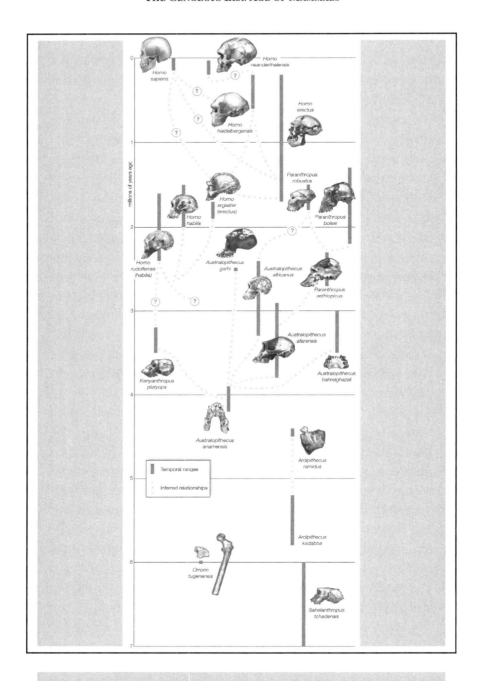

Possible pathways in the evolution of the human lineage. Encyclopædia Britannica, Inc.

Asia and across the narrow seaways of Java, the Sunda Islands, and New Guinea to Australia by at least 40,000 years ago. Spread of humans into the New World was delayed until possibly as late as 11,000 years ago, but there is controversial evidence for earlier colonization. A wealth of evidence is available in Europe for the development of human technology and culture during the Upper Paleolithic through Neolithic cultural stages, ranging from the skillfully crafted stone, bone, and wooden tools found in many locations to rare but revealing cave art. These artifacts can be interpreted in various ways, but they clearly were the product of intelligent and emotionally complex humans.

It is probably no coincidence that after the strictures imposed by cold and rapidly changing Pleistocene climates and landscapes, human civilization and recorded history arose during the more amenable climate of the Holocene. However, even in these quieter times, vast climate and sea-level disruptions have occurred. In the late 1990s evidence of catastrophic flooding of the Black Sea was discovered. The event took place approximately 8,000 years ago and would have flooded settlements and displaced peoples, possibly accelerating the dispersal of Neolithic foragers and farmers into Europe.

Vivid cave paintings, such as those in Lascaux, France, as well as rock engravings in Australia and many other parts of the world, depict bison, antelope, horse, mammoth, and other animals with which humans interacted during the Late Pleistocene. Many tools were obviously intended for hunting both large and small game. Other tools are interpreted as specialized scrapers for hides and awls for sewing skins. Rare finds of mammoth and other animals with stone points embedded in the bones or closely associated with the skeletons attest to animal hunting. In addition, camps in Siberia have tent circles

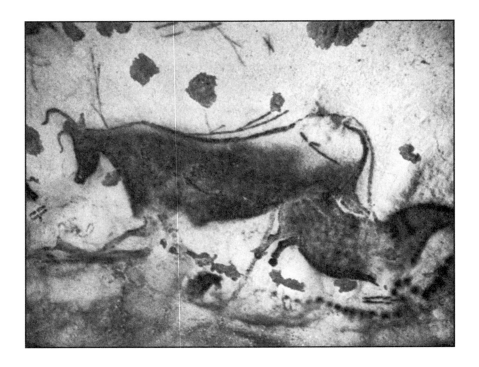

Cave painting of a bull and a horse; in Lascaux Grotto, near Montignac, France. Hans Hinz, Basel

composed of woolly mammoth jaws and tusks. These could have come from either hunted or scavenged animals. Like Stone Age peoples known from recent centuries, these hunter-gatherers used the meat, bones, hides, and sinews of animals, along with many plants, for food, tools, and shelter. Clearly, these animal resources were critical to survival, especially in the cold regions.

QUATERNARY GEOLOGY

Quaternary sediments are widespread on the ocean floor and on the continents. There are few places where sands and mud have piled up in thick enough accumulations to become lithified, but on reefs and lagoons, tropical shelves, and other areas where cementation is rapid, true Quaternary-age rock occurs. A striking aspect of Quaternary sediments is that many occur in recognizable association with landforms and environments in which they were produced. Thus, Quaternary lake shorelines and sediments are associated with modern remnant lakes, as at the Great Salt Lake in Utah, a remnant of Lake Bonneville. Glacial moraines at the mouth of Alpine and Rocky Mountain valleys can easily be seen as preserved ancient examples of moraines forming at higher elevations today. Large marine delta deposits of Quaternary age are often associated with the same major rivers that are still actively building their modern deltas, such as the Mississippi River and Ganges River deltas. These close associations with modern environments and processes allow confident interpretation of the Quaternary systems and provide a framework for interpretation of more ancient rocks.

THE ECONOMIC SIGNIFICANCE OF QUATERNARY DEPOSITS

Most of the world's soils are formed on Quaternary sediments, forming the breadbasket of the North American central plains. Much of this abundance comes from the vast floors of former glacial lakes, such as Lake Agassiz in North America and the windblown glacial-age dust that accumulated as thick layers of silt called loess. Streams and rivers reworked these primary deposits to shape the vast floodplains and deltas of the Missouri and Mississippi rivers of the United States, the Huang He and the Yangtze River (Chang Jiang) of China, the Rhine valley of Europe, and others around the world. Deposits of sand and gravel left by melting glaciers are crucial raw materials for civil engineering and construction projects worldwide. Sand and gravel are also extracted from Quaternary marine and fluvial terraces, former shorelines, and even offshore on the continental shelf. Quaternary sea-level changes and shoreline migrations modified the surface of continental shelves and nearshore basins that define bottom-fishing areas. For example, the Gulf of Maine, Georges Bank, Scotian Shelf and Gulf of St. Lawrence, the Grand Banks, and the Irish, Celtic, and North seas were all affected by sea-level changes and, in some cases, direct glacial activity that produced the variable seafloor types and deflections of currents that result in highly productive fisheries.

Extensive groundwater supplies lie within Quaternary sediments. Occasionally, valuable minerals are found in Quaternary sediments. For example, gold and diamond placer deposits are found in stream gravels and beaches. The 1849 California Gold Rush started from such a deposit at Sutter's Mill, and gold is still mined from placers in Alaska. In the United States, the greatest economic benefit of Quaternary sediments is in land for homes and recreational retreats. Much of the coastline of the eastern and southern United States is coastal sand brought by the glaciers or through changing sea levels during the period. When observed at geologic time scales, shorelines are constantly in motion, and ephemeral shifting is perceived even over the course of human lives.

TYPES OF QUATERNARY SEDIMENTS

Quaternary sediments are commonly recognized in the field by their lack of consolidation into rock and by association with landforms representing processes of deposition (river terraces, shorelines, moraines, and drumlins, for example). The fossils in these deposits are similar to modern life-forms, but they may represent evidence of cooler (or sometimes warmer) climates. Quaternary sediments are most easily distinguished in temperate latitudes where glacial or periglacial processes held sway. Till is a distinctive type in many locations. This poorly sorted mix of debris contains a fine matrix enclosing outsized pebbles, cobbles, boulders, and sometimes rock types carried from distant locations (erratics). Boulder-strewn ridges and blankets of till in central North America or the northern European plains contain erratics carried for hundreds of kilometres from their source, indicating deposition from a continental ice sheet.

Glacial erratic perched on low pedestal of massive granite, Tulare County, Calif. Courtesy of the U.S. Geological Survey, Washington, D.C.

It seems self-evident today, but prior to the early 1800s most scientists thought till formations were deposits of the biblical flood, perhaps carried by icebergs. The term "drift," used generically to describe glacial sediment, is an anachronism from this time. However, European and Scandinavian scientists (and laypeople as well) noticed the similarity to Alpine glacier deposits. In 1840 Swiss scientist Louis Agassiz formulated a sweeping theory of ice ages and extensive continental ice sheets to explain these deposits. Later emigrating to the United States and becoming a professor at Harvard, Agassiz vigorously promoted this theory, which has evolved into our present understanding.

Glacial marine and glacial lake sediments are common near shorelines that were affected by climatic, sea-level, or rebound effects. Glacial lake sediments are often much richer in sand, silt, and clay, and they contain less organic material than Holocene lake sediments. They may be strongly laminated, with rhythmic alteration of light coarse-grained layers and darker fine-grained layers of less than a millimetre to a few centimetres thick. This rhythmic lamination often represents a seasonal cycle, in which case the laminae are called varves. If the seasonal cycle can be confidently accepted, varves provide excellent correlation tools and function as a measure of time independent of radiometric techniques. Glacial marine sediments may be laminated, but they are most often characterized by dropstones (ice-rafted debris of pebble to boulder size) that were carried by icebergs into the ocean.

Loess is silt that is picked up by high winds in areas that lack vegetation. This Quaternary sediment accumulated in thick blankets away from the edges of ice sheets. Much of the northern Mississippi River valley, northern China, and the extensive plains of Asia and northern Europe are blanketed by loess.

Carbonate platform and shelf environments, such as in Florida, the Bahamas, the Great Barrier Reef, and many other tropical shorelines were strongly affected by lowered sea levels. Sea levels more than 100 metres (300 feet) below today's resulted in exposed bank tops. Some of these were eroded by rainwater into extensive cave systems, while in some areas winds blew the exposed carbonates into extensive dune ridges. When the sea level rose again, the caves were filled with water, creating spectacular grottoes found by divers in Florida, the Bahamas, and Central America. The bank tops were submerged at the latest stages, and the dune ridges remained to form the core of the modern Bahamas, Bermuda, and many other such islands.

THE CORRELATION OF QUATERNARY DEPOSITS

Correlation of Quaternary terrestrial sedimentary deposits has long been a challenge. It is easy in some areas to map terminal moraines as they trace across the landscapes of Indiana and Ohio, or from Denmark through northern Germany into Poland and Lithuania. However, correlation of glacial and interglacial events from continent to continent and between hemispheres requires extensive radiometric dating of fossils. The advent of marine oxygen isotopic records gave fresh impetus to attempts to correlate the long-held "four glaciation" models from various parts of the Northern Hemisphere. More important, isotopic records have shown that there were actually as many as 30 distinct glaciations and many shorter events within the Pleistocene alone. In the 1990s a new global viewpoint emerged from the extremely detailed record preserved in ice cores from Greenland, Antarctica, and smaller glaciers around the world. There are differences among these cores, but in general the records show many of the same features as the marine record and the more traditional pollen records and glacial sediment maps. Ice cores allow counting of annual layers for much of the record. Distinctive isotopic events correlate to marine records that can be directly dated with radiocarbon or other radiometric techniques. Correlation from place to place on the globe is thus facilitated by this ice core scale.

Marine sediments have been somewhat easier to correlate based on microfossils of foraminifera or diatoms. Recognition of shifts in ocean currents and temperature bands comes through analysis of many cores along transects of the world's oceans. In some areas, distinct events provide distinct marker horizons. For instance, near Iceland and in the Mediterranean, volcanic ash horizons provide clear markers that are simultaneous in many cores. These can be correlated to radiometric dates and can also be found on land and in ice cores. Thus, the marine, terrestrial, and ice-core records can be tied together. One of the best-known examples of volcanic ash serving as an "instantaneous" marker horizon is the Bishop Tuff, erupted from the Long Valley Caldera in California about 740,000 years ago. This ash is found in Pleistocene sediments as far away as eastern Nebraska. Along with other ashes, the Bishop Tuff can be identified by its chemistry and confidently dated with radiometric techniques such as potassium-argon and argon-40–argon-39 dating.

SIGNIFICANT LIFE-FORMS OF THE QUATERNARY PERIOD

Because Quaternary time encompasses the most recent 2.6 million years, it is conceivable that all modern forms of life could be incorporated into this section along with such recently extinct species as the dodo (*Raphus cucullatus*), the thylacine (*Thylacinus cynocephalus*), and the passenger pigeon (*Ectopistes migratorius*). The groups described in the following text, however, belong to a collection of animals that died out before the advent of writing. Many types, such as *Casteroides*, *Megatherium*, and *Mylodon*, were larger relatives of modern species.

AEPYORNIS

Aepyornis is an extinct genus of giant flightless birds found as fossils in Pleistocene and post-Pleistocene deposits (the Pleistocene Epoch began 2.6 million years ago and ended 11,700 years ago) on the island of Madagascar. The remains of *Aepyornis* are abundant, and several known species were massively constructed. With conical beaks, short, thick legs, three-toed feet, and relatively small wings that were useless for flight, the birds were probably slow-moving inhabitants of forests. Some forms of *Aepyornis* attained very large size; *Aepyornis titan,* or *maximus,* stood 3 metres (10 feet) high and weighed about 450 kg (1,000 pounds). The skull in *Aepyornis* was small, and the neck was long and slim.

The fossilized remains of *Aepyornis* eggs are relatively common, both fragmented and intact. The eggs of the giant forms were apparently the largest eggs ever laid by any animal. One of the largest intact specimens is 89 cm (35 inches) in circumference around its long axis and probably had a capacity of about 9 litres (more than 2 gallons). A few *Aepyornis* eggs contain the bones of embryonic young.

Although *Aepyornis* occurred relatively late in the geologic record, it was a primitive member of the ratites, an evolutionary lineage that includes the ostrich, rhea, and emu. *Aepyornis* species survived on Madagascar well into the period of the island's human occupation. The birds became extinct sometime in the last 1,000 years, probably as a result of hunting and habitat loss caused by deforestation. *Aepyornis* may have given rise to the Arabic legend of the roc, a gigantic bird. Colloquially, members of *Aepyornis* are often called elephant birds.

CASTOROIDES

Castoroides is an extinct genus of giant beavers found as fossils in Pleistocene deposits in North America. Members of this genus attained a length of about 2.5 metres (7.5 feet). The skull was large and the gnawing teeth strongly developed. In Europe a similar form of giant beaver, *Trogontherium,* paralleled the development of *Castoroides.*

Diprotodon

Diprotodon is an extinct genus of giant marsupials found as fossils in Pleistocene deposits in Australia. *Diprotodon,* the largest marsupial known, reached a length of about 3½ metres (11 feet) and was nearly as massive as a large rhinoceros. The limbs and skeleton were massively constructed to support its imposing bulk. The well-developed incisor teeth resemble those of gnawing animals. *Diprotodon* became extinct at the close of the Pleistocene.

Dire Wolf

The dire wolf (*Canis dirus*) is a species of wolf that existed during the Pleistocene Epoch. It is probably the most common mammalian species to be found preserved in the La Brea Tar Pits in southern California. The dire wolf differed from the modern wolf in several ways: it was larger and it had a more massive skull, a smaller brain, and relatively light limbs. The species was considerably widespread, and skeletal remains have been found in Florida, the Mississippi Valley, and the Valley of Mexico.

Irish Elk

The Irish elk (*Megaloceros giganteus*), also known as the Irish or giant deer, is an extinct species of deer, characterized by immense body size and wide antlers, commonly found as fossils in Pleistocene deposits in Europe and Asia. Despite its distribution throughout Eurasia, the species was most abundant in Ireland. Although several other species of *Megaloceros* are known, the Irish elk was the largest. It was about the size of the modern moose (*Alces alces*) and had the largest antlers of any form of deer known—in some specimens, 4 metres (about 13 feet)

Dire wolf (Canis dirus) *from Rancho La Brea, Calif.; detail of a mural by Charles R. Knight, 1922.* Courtesy of the American Museum of Natural History, New York

across. The antlers differed from those of the modern deer: the main part was a massive single sheet from which arose a series of pointed projections, or tines.

Many scientists contend that the Irish elk succumbed to starvation and went extinct during the most recent ice age. Fossils of *M. giganteus* uncovered in Siberia have been dated to approximately 7,000–8,000 years ago, however, a period characterized by warm temperatures.

MAMMOTH

The name "mammoth" refers to any member of an extinct group of elephants of the genus *Mammuthus* found as fossils in Pleistocene deposits over every continent except Australia and South America and in early Holocene deposits of North America. (The Holocene Epoch began 11,700 years ago and continues through the present.) The woolly, Northern, or Siberian mammoth (*M. primigenius*) is by far the best-known of all mammoths. The relative abundance and, at times, excellent preservation of this species' carcasses found in the permanently frozen ground of Siberia has provided much information about mammoths' structure and habits. Fossil mammoth ivory was previously so abundant that it was exported from Siberia to China and Europe from medieval times. Scientific evidence suggests that small populations of woolly mammoths in North America may have survived until between 10,500 and 7,600 years ago.

Mammoths figured significantly in the art of primitive humans, and cave dwellers in Europe realistically depicted herds of these animals. Mammoths were sometimes trapped in ice crevasses and covered over. When they were frozen, their bodies were so remarkably well preserved that cases have been reported in which sled dogs actually were fed the meat from frozen mammoth carcasses that had begun to thaw out of the ice that had held them for almost 30,000 years.

A variety of distinct species are included in the genus *Mammuthus*. Most mammoths were about as large as modern elephants, the North American imperial mammoth (*M. imperator*) attaining a shoulder height of 4 metres (14 feet). At the other extreme were certain dwarfed forms whose ancestors became isolated on various islands. Many mammoths had a woolly, yellowish brown undercoat about 2.5 cm (1 inch) thick beneath a coarser outer covering of dark brown hair up to 50 cm (20 inches) long. Under the extremely thick skin was a layer of insulating fat at times 8 cm (3 inches) thick. The skull in *Mammuthus* was high and domelike. The ears, small for an elephant, were probably adaptively advantageous for an animal living in a cold climate, because the smaller amount of exposed surface area diminished heat losses. A mound of fat present as a hump on the back is lacking in fossil remains, but evidence for its presence comes from cave paintings. The prominent tusks were directed downward and were long, older males sometimes sporting tusks that curved over each other. Mammoth dentition was made up of alternating plates of enamel and a denture that often became worn down by constant back-to-front chewing motions. Remains of arctic plants have been found in the digestive tracts of frozen mammoth carcasses. It is clear that the mammoth was hunted by early North American hunters.

MEGATHERIUM

The largest of the ground sloths belonged to the genus *Megatherium*, an extinct group of mammals belonging to a group containing sloths, anteaters, glyptodonts, and armadillos that underwent a highly successful evolutionary radiation in South America in the Cenozoic Era. The size of these animals approximated that of a modern elephant, and they were equipped with large claws and teeth, the latter confined to the sides of the jaw, because the animal fed largely on the leaves of trees and bushes. Ground sloths briefly appeared in North America during the Pleistocene Epoch, when a land connection was established between the American continents.

MYLODON

Mylodon is an extinct genus of ground sloth found as fossils in South American deposits of the Pleistocene Epoch. *Mylodon* attained a length of about 3 metres (10 feet).

Megatherium. Encyclopædia Britannica, Inc.

Although its skin contained numerous bony parts that offered some protection against the attacks of predators, *Mylodon* remains found in cave deposits in association with human artifacts suggest that people hunted and ate them.

Mylodon probably subsisted on the foliage of trees and shrubs. Well-developed claws were probably used to dig up tubers or hold branches while the animal stripped them of leaves. *Mylodon* and its relatives were the dominant group of South American ground sloths and are distinguished from other ground sloths by the presence of upper canine teeth, triangular cheek teeth, and a small first toe on the hind limbs. Two closely related genera, *Paramylodon* and *Glossotherium*, were widely distributed and even spread into many regions of North America.

Mylodon, *an extinct genus of giant ground sloth.* Encyclopædia Britannica, Inc.

TOXODON

Toxodon is an extinct genus of mammals of the late Pliocene and the Pleistocene Epoch in South America that is representative of an extinct family of animals, the Toxodontidae. This family was at its most diverse during the Miocene Epoch (23 million to 5.3 million years ago). About 2.75 metres (9 feet) long and about 1.5 metres (5 feet) high at the shoulder, *Toxodon* resembled a short rhinoceros. Nasal openings on top of the skull indicate a large, well-developed snout, and the incisors were separated from each other by large gaps and from the cheek teeth by even larger gaps. The massive skeleton suggests that it supported a large, heavy body. The feet were short and broad and had three functional toes, with major stresses directed through the axis of the central toe.

Toxodon was probably the most common large hoofed mammal in South America during the Pleistocene Epoch. On his famous voyage aboard HMS *Beagle*, English naturalist Charles Darwin collected fossil specimens of *Toxodon*, which were subsequently described by British anatomist and paleontologist Richard Owen. Because *Toxodon* indicated that the fossil mammals of South America were different from those of Europe, it figured prominently in late 19th-century debates about evolution.

WOOLLY RHINOCEROS

The woolly rhinoceros (*Coelodonta antiquitatis*) is an extinct species of rhinoceros found in fossil deposits of the Pleistocene Epoch in Europe, North Africa, and Asia. It probably evolved from an earlier form, *Dicerorhinus*, somewhere in northeastern Asia, entered the European region, and became extinct at the end of the most recent ice age. Frozen carcasses of woolly rhinoceroses have been found preserved in Siberia, and others have been found well preserved in oil seeps in central Europe. The animal was massive, with two large horns toward the front of the skull, and covered with a thick coat of hair.

The woolly rhinoceros was also present in more temperate, nonglacial regions, where it inhabited grasslands. It was a popular subject for Stone Age painters and sculptors. Their representations of the woolly rhinoceros, some of which are quite accurate, are known from several localities.

CHAPTER 6

THE PLEISTOCENE EPOCH

The Pleistocene Epoch, the earlier of the two epochs that constitute the Quaternary Period of the Earth's history, is also known as the time period during which a succession of glacial and interglacial climatic cycles occurred. The base of the Gelasian Stage (2,588,000 to 1,800,000 years ago) marks the beginning of Pleistocene, which is also the base of the Quaternary Period. It is coincident with the bottom of a marly layer resting atop a sapropel (a loose sedimentary deposit rich in bituminous material) called MPRS 250 on the southern slopes of Monte San Nicola in Sicily, Italy, and is associated with the Gauss-Matuyama geomagnetic reversal. The Pleistocene ended 11,700 years ago. It is preceded by the Pliocene Epoch of the Neogene Period and is followed by the Holocene Epoch.

The Pleistocene Epoch is best known as a time during which extensive ice sheets and other glaciers formed repeatedly on the landmasses and has been informally referred to as the "Great Ice Age." The timing of the onset of this cold interval, and thus the formal beginning of the Pleistocene Epoch, was a matter of substantial debate among geologists during the late 20th and early 21st centuries. Although by 1985 many geological societies agreed to set the beginning of the Pleistocene Epoch about 1,800,000 years ago, a figure coincident with the onset of glaciation in Europe and North America, modern research has shown that large glaciers had formed in other parts of

the world earlier than 1,800,000 years ago. This fact pre-
cipitated a debate among geologists over the formal start
of the Pleistocene, as well as the status of the Quaternary
Period, that was not resolved until 2009.

PLEISTOCENE STRATIGRAPHY

The chronology of the Pleistocene originally developed
through observation and study of the glacial succession,
which in both Europe and the United States was found to
contain either soils that developed under warm climatic
conditions or marine deposits enclosed between glacial
deposits. From these studies, as well as studies of river
terraces in the Alps, a chronology was developed that suggested the Pleistocene consisted of four or five major
glacial stages which were separated by interglacial stages
with climates generally similar to those of today. Beginning
with studies in the 1950s, a much better chronology and
record of Pleistocene climatic events have evolved through
analyses of deep-sea sediments, particularly from the oxygen isotope record of the shells of microorganisms that
lived in the oceans. In addition, loess deposits, glacial
records, and ice cores help scientists better describe the
climatic conditions of the Pleistocene.

THE MARINE OXYGEN ISOTOPE RECORD

The isotopic record is based on the ratio of two oxygen
isotopes, oxygen-16 (^{16}O) and oxygen-18 (^{18}O), which is
determined on calcium carbonate from shells of microfossils that accumulated year by year on the seafloor. The
ratio depends on two factors, the temperature and the isotopic composition of the seawater from which the
organism secreted its shell. Shells secreted from colder

water contain more ^{18}O relative to ^{16}O than do shells secreted from warmer water. The isotopic composition of the oceans has proved to be related to the storage of water in large ice sheets on land. Because molecules of ^{18}O evaporate less readily and condense more readily, an air mass with oceanic water vapour becomes depleted in the heavier isotope (^{18}O) as the air mass is cooled and loses water by precipitation. When moisture condenses and falls as snow, its isotopic composition is also dependent on the temperature of the air. Snow falling on a large ice sheet becomes isotopically lighter (that is, has less ^{18}O) as one goes higher on the glacier surface where it is both colder and farther from the moisture source. As a result, large ice sheets store water that is relatively light (has more ^{16}O), and so during a major glaciation the ocean waters become relatively heavier (contain more ^{18}O) than during interglacial times when there is less global ice. Accordingly, the shells of marine organisms that formed during a glaciation contain more ^{18}O than those that formed during an interglaciation. Although the exact relationship is unknown, about 70 percent of the isotopic change in shell carbonate is the result of changes in the isotopic composition of seawater. Because the latter is directly related to the volume of ice on land, the marine oxygen isotope record is primarily a record of past glaciations on the continents.

Long core samples taken in portions of the ocean where sedimentation rates were high and generally continuous and where water temperature changes were relatively small have revealed a long record of oxygen isotope changes that indicate repeated glaciations and interglaciations going back to the Pliocene. The record is relatively consistent from one core sample to the next and can be correlated throughout the oceans. Warmer periods (interglacials) are assigned odd numbers with the current warm interval, the Holocene, being 1, while the colder glacial periods are assigned even numbers. Subdivisions within isotopic stages are delineated by letters. Although the ages of the stage boundaries cannot be measured directly, they can be estimated from available radiometric ages of the cores and from position with respect to both paleomagnetic boundaries and biostratigraphic markers and also by using sedimentation rates relative to these data.

The record for the last 730,000 years indicates that eight major glacial and interglacial events or climatic cycles of about 100,000 years' duration occurred during this interval. An isotopic record from the North Atlantic suggests the first major glaciation in that region occurred about 2,400,000 years ago. It also suggests that the first glaciation likely to have covered extensive areas of North America and Eurasia occurred about 850,000 years ago during oxygen isotope stage 22. The largest glaciations appear to have taken place during stages 2, 6, 12, and 16. The interglacials with the least global ice, and thus possibly the warmest, appear to be stages 1, 5, 9, and 11. The last interglaciation occurred during all of stage 5 or just substage 5e, depending on location; the last glaciation took place during stages 4, 3, and 2; and the current interglaciation falls during stage 1.

The marine isotopic record is a continuous record, unlike most terrestrial records, which contain gaps because of erosion or lack of sedimentation and soil formation or a combination of these factors. Because of its continuity and excellent record of climatic events on land (glaciations), the marine oxygen isotope record is the standard to which the terrestrial and other stratigraphic records are correlated. Correlations to it are based on available chronometric ages, paleomagnetic data where available, and attempts to match the terrestrial record and its interpretation with specific characteristics of the isotopic curve. Unfortunately, most terrestrial records contain few radiometric ages and are incomplete, and specific correlations, except for the most recent part of the record, are difficult and uncertain. A few terrestrial records, however, are exceptional and can be correlated with confidence.

LOESS-PALEOSOL RECORDS

Central China is covered by deposits of windblown dust and silt, called loess. Locally, the loess is more than 100 metres (300 feet) thick, mantling hillsides and forming

With minimal erosion, a succession of windblown silt and dust, known as loess, provides a particularly informative chronological record. G. R. 'Dick' Roberts/NSIL/Visuals Unlimited/Getty Images

loess plateaus and tablelands. The loess accumulated primarily during times that were colder and drier than present, and most of it was derived from desert areas to the west. The loess succession contains many colourful buried soils or paleosols that formed during periods that were both warmer and wetter than today. Thus, on stable tablelands with minimal erosion, the succession provides an exceptional climatic and chronological record that extends back 2.4 million years to the late Pliocene. In total, up to 44 climatic cycles have been delineated, with more frequent cycles occurring during the early Pleistocene. Although indirectly related to glaciation, correlation with the marine oxygen isotope record is excellent, and many specific loess and soil units have similar climatic inferences, as do their correlative ^{18}O stages.

Another loess–paleosol succession occurs in the Czech Republic, Slovakia, and Austria, where loess blankets terraces of the major rivers that drained eastward and southward from the principal glaciated areas in the Alps and northern Europe. As in China, buried soils are common in the loess succession and, along with gastropod shells, provide paleoclimatic data and evidence for climatic change. The climatic cycles varied from cold and dry conditions when loess accumulated to warm and wet conditions with hardwood forests and well-developed soils. In the last 730,000 years, eight climatic cycles have been delineated, which correlate with the eight ^{18}O cycles that occurred in the marine record during the same time interval. During the entire Pleistocene, about 17 glacial episodes alternated with 17 interglacials.

GLACIAL RECORDS

Glacial till, which was directly deposited by glaciers, covers extensive areas of northern Eurasia and northern

North America and occurs as well in many mountain regions and other areas that currently are not covered by glacial ice. Soils of warm climate origin buried between tills were recognized long ago and provided the basis for the development of the idea of multiple glaciation during the Pleistocene. Because direct dating of the deposits generally is not possible and the glacial sequence is not complete as a result of erosion or nondeposition or a combination of the two, however, the development of long chronological records and correlation to the ^{18}O record are difficult. Correlations generally are possible for the last two climatic cycles. They also are feasible in areas where the glacial succession contains interbedded volcanic rocks from which radiometric ages can be obtained.

In the mid-continental region of the United States, early work recognized tills that were interpreted to represent four major glaciations and three major buried soils that were viewed as representing interglaciations. Subsequent work showed that the glaciated record was more complex and that parts of the older record were miscorrelated. Consequently, the older portion of the record is informally referred to as the pre-Illinoian, and the older glacial and interglacial terms are no longer used except locally. Volcanic ash occurs within the succession in Iowa, Kansas, and Nebraska and is useful for correlation and dating. In one core, till occurs below ash that has been dated at about 2.2 million years old, suggesting late Pliocene glaciation. Other tills of the pre-Illinoian sequence probably are correlative with ^{18}O stages 22, 16, and 12, and possibly others. The Illinoian correlates with ^{18}O stage 6 and possibly stage 8, and the Sangamonian correlates with stage 5.

The last glacial interval, the Wisconsinan, is subdivided into three parts, an early stage (substage) of glaciation, a middle interstadial, or time of restricted

CLASSIC GLACIAL/COLD AND INTERGLACIAL/ WARM EPISODES*			
OXYGEN-18 STAGE	CENTRAL UNITED STATES	GREAT BRITAIN	NORTHWESTERN EUROPE
1	Holocene	Holocene, Flandrian	Holocene, Flandrian
	Wisconsinan	Devensian	Weichselian
2	late	late	late
3	middle	middle	middle
4 or 5a-d	early	early	early
5 or 5e	**Sangamonian**	**Ipswichian**	**Eemian**
6, 8?	Illinoian	Wolstonian	Saalian
6			Warthe
8			Drenthe
	Yarmouthian**	**Hoxnian**	**Holsteinian**
12	Kansan**	Anglian	Elsterian
	Aftonian**	**Cromerian**	**Cromerian complex**
	Nebraskan**	Beestonian	**Bavel complex**
		Pastonian	
		Pre-Pastonian	Menapian
		Bramertonian	**Waalian**
		Baventian	Eburonian
		Antian	**Tiglian**
		Thurnian	
		Ludhamian	
		Pre-Ludhamian?	Pretiglian

*Interglacial/warm episodes in boldface; correlations between areas are not well established and are not intended for the early portion of the record.
**Included informally in the pre-Illinoian.

glaciation, and a late stade of glaciation. These intervals generally correlate with ^{18}O stages 4, 3, and 2, respectively. Deposits of the early and middle Wisconsinan are poorly known in the mid-continental region of the United States, so the area probably was not glaciated. Tills of the early Wisconsinan and even some that are correlative with ^{18}O substages 5d or 5b, however, are common in the Canadian Arctic and on Baffin Island, where the ice sheet developed much earlier. It was not until the late Wisconsinan, about 18,000 years ago, that the southern ice sheet margin reached its maximum extent in the United States and eastern and western Canada. The ice sheet margin began to retreat and downwaste (thin out) soon after reaching its maximum position, and the United States was deglaciated by about 10,000 years ago. Hudson Bay, near the centre of the ice sheet, was open to the ocean by 8,000 years ago, and, except for the Barnes and Penny ice caps on Baffin Island, the ice sheet had dissipated from the upland areas of central Canada by 6,000 years ago, well into the Holocene and ^{18}O stage 1.

A somewhat similar chronology has been developed for the glaciated areas of Eurasia and the British Isles based on a variety of criteria. In addition to tills and buried soils, marine deposits, permafrost features, and fossil pollen and beetles have been used to subdivide the succession on a climatic basis. As elsewhere, the earlier portion of the record is not well established, and correlations among different geographic areas, as well as to the marine ^{18}O record, are uncertain. The first cold period, known as the Pretiglian and based on pollen data from the Netherlands, began about 2.3 million years ago, soon after extensive ice-rafted material first appears in North Atlantic deep-sea cores.

The Pretiglian was followed by a succession of warm and cold intervals, which also are based on pollen and on other flora and fauna evidence and which have been given different names in different areas. Although several old gravels with glacial erratics are known, the oldest major glacial episodes with extensive till deposits are the Elsterian in northern Germany and the Anglian in England. These glaciations probably are correlative with ¹⁸O stage 12, and local evidence suggests the possibility of earlier glacial events. Along coastal areas, these tills are overlain by the marine Holstein deposits, which also may represent more than one high sea-level stand.

The next major glacial sequence is the Saalian of Germany, which is subdivided into the Drenthe and the Warthe, which probably correlate with ¹⁸O stages 8 and 6, respectively. Deposits and soils of the last interglaciation, the Eemian and Ipswichian, are correlative with ¹⁸O stage 5e, and those of the last glaciation, the Weichselian and Devensian, correlate with ¹⁸O stages 5d–a, 4, 3, and 2. As in central North America, tills and other deposits are well known only from the last part of this interval. The deglacial history generally is similar, except for a widespread but short interval of renewed glacial activity and cold climatic conditions that is known as the Younger Dryas in Scandinavia and Loch Lomond in the British Isles. This event occurred about 11,000 years ago, some 2,000 years before the dissipation of the ice sheet.

ICE-CORE RECORDS

A relatively short but important late Pleistocene and Holocene climatic record is derived from ice cores that have been taken from the ice sheets of Antarctica, Greenland, and Arctic Canada. The ice record in several cores extends back to the last interglaciation (¹⁸O stage 5) and, in one case, to the next-to-the-last glaciation (stage 6). Although dating of the lower portions of the ice cores is difficult, annual layers of snow and ice can be counted in the upper parts and an accurate time scale reconstructed. Because the air temperature at the time when moisture condenses to fall as snow controls the oxygen and hydrogen isotopic composition of the snow, investigators are able to reconstruct temperature variations through isotopic studies of the ice cores. Data from the Vostok core taken from the East Antarctic Ice Sheet indicate that the climatic record of the Southern Hemisphere is similar to that interpreted from Northern Hemisphere records with respect to times of glaciation and interglaciation.

It also is possible to measure the amount of microparticles (extremely fine dust) in the ice, and studies of this kind show that there are many more particles in the portions of the core that accumulated during periods of extensive glaciation, apparently reflecting greater atmospheric circulation and dust in the atmosphere at those times. Trapped air preserved in small bubbles in the ice gives an indication of the composition of the atmosphere at the time the ice (snow) accumulated. An important result from this work indicates that the amount of carbon dioxide in the atmosphere during the last glacial (stages 2, 3, and 4) was substantially less than during the Holocene (stage 1) and the last interglaciation (stage 5e). This observation has significant implications with respect to climate and climatic change during glacial and interglacial transitions.

THE PLIOCENE–PLEISTOCENE BOUNDARY

Definition of the base of the Pleistocene has had a long and controversial history. Because the epoch is best recognized for glaciation and climatic change, many have suggested that its lower boundary should be based on climatic criteria (for example, the oldest glacial deposits or the first occurrence of a fossil of a cold-climate life-form in the sediment record). Other criteria that have been used to define the Pliocene–Pleistocene include the appearance of humans, the appearance of certain vertebrate fossils in Europe, and the appearance or extinction of certain microfossils in deep-sea sediments. These criteria continue to be considered locally, and some workers advocate a climatic boundary at about 2.4 million years.

Pre-Pleistocene intervals of time are defined on the basis of chronostratigraphic and geochronologic principles related to a marine sequence of strata. Following studies by a series of international working groups, correlation programs, and stratigraphic commissions, agreement was reached in 1985 to place the lower boundary of the Pleistocene series at the base of marine claystones that conformably overlie a specific marker bed in the Vrica section in Calabria. The boundary occurs near the level of several important marine biostratigraphic events and, more significantly, is just above the position of the magnetic reversal that marks the top of the Olduvai Normal Polarity Subzone, thus allowing worldwide correlation.

Because evidence of Cenozoic glaciation was discovered in rocks laid down earlier than those of the Vrica section, some geologists proposed that the base of the Pleistocene be moved to an earlier time. To many geologists, the most reasonable time coincided with the type section for the Gelasian Stage, the rock layer laid down during the Gelasian Age, found at Monte San Nicola near Gela, Sicily. The base marker for the Gelasian (that is, the Global Stratotype Section and Point [GSSP]) was placed in rock dated to 2,588,000 years ago (a notable point because it is within 20,000 years of the Gauss-Matuyama geomagnetic reversal). In addition, the date of the rock is closely correlated with the timing of a substantial change in the size of granules found in Chinese loess deposits. (Changes in loess grain size suggest regional climate changes.) After years of discussion, the International Union of Geological Sciences (IUGS) and the International Commission on Stratigraphy (ICS) designated the Gelasian as the lowermost stage of the Pleistocene Epoch.

STAGES OF THE PLEISTOCENE EPOCH

The Pleistocene is subdivided into four ages and their corresponding rock units: the Gelasian (2.6 million to 1.8 million years ago), the Calabrian (1.8 million to 780,000 years ago), the Ionian (780,000 to 126,000 years ago), and the Tarantian (126,000 to 11,700 years ago). Of these, only the Gelasian and Calabrian are formal intervals, whereas others await ratification by the ICS. The Calabrian, which was previously known as the early Pleistocene, extends to the Brunhes-Matuyama paleomagnetic boundary at 780,000 years ago. The Ionian, also known as the middle Pleistocene, extends to the end of the next to the last glaciation at about 130,000 years ago. The Tarantian, also known as the late Pleistocene, includes the last interglacial–glacial cycle ending at the Holocene boundary about 11,700 years ago.

GELASIAN STAGE

The Gelasian Stage is the first of four stages of the Pleistocene Series, encompassing all rocks deposited during the Gelasian Age (2.588 million to 1.806 million years ago) of the Pleistocene Epoch in the Quaternary Period. The name of this interval is derived from the town of Gela in Sicily, Italy.

In 1996 the ICS established the GSSP defining the base of this unit in the marly shales on the southern slope of Monte San Nicola near Gela. The shales sit atop a sapropel of the Mediterranean Precession Related Sapropels (MPRS) 250 layer. The marker is located about 1 metre (3 feet) above the strata indicative of the Gauss-Matuyama paleomagnetic boundary and slightly below the final occurrence of *Discoaster pentaradiatus*, a calcareous nannofossil. (Calcareous nannofossils are the remains of ocean-dwelling golden-brown algae composed of calcite platelets.)

This GSSP also specifies the base of the Pleistocene Series and the Quaternary System. Formerly, the Gelasian was the third and final stage of the Pliocene Series, and the beginning of the Pleistocene was demarcated by the base of the Calabrian Stage. In 2009 the IUGS ratified the decision to make the base of the Pleistocene coincident with the base of the Gelasian. The Gelasian Stage overlies the Piacenzian Stage of the Pliocene Series and underlies the Calabrian Stage.

CALABRIAN STAGE

The Calabrian Stage, the second of four stages of the Pleistocene Series, represents all rocks deposited during the Calabrian Age (1.8 million to 781,000 years ago) of the Quaternary Period. The name of this interval is derived from the region of the same name in southern Italy.

As defined in 1985, the GSSP for its lower boundary is the base of claystones in a sequence of marine strata about 4 km (2.5 miles) south of Crotone on the Marchesato Peninsula of Calabria, Italy. The upper boundary of the Calabrian Stage has not been agreed upon universally. Some geologists consider the Calabrian to encompass all rocks laid down during the entire Pleistocene, which was succeeded by the Holocene Epoch approximately 11,700 years ago. Other geologists consider the Calabrian to be an alternate name for the Lower Pleistocene Stage, which is overlain by the Ionian, or Middle Pleistocene, Stage at a boundary laid down some 780,000 years ago. In neither case has a GSSP been agreed upon for the upper boundary of the Calabrian Stage.

Until 2009 the base of the Calabrian defined the beginning of the Pleistocene Epoch. The IUGS has since ratified the decision to make the base of the Pleistocene Epoch coincident with the base of the Gelasian Stage.

IONIAN STAGE

The Ionian Stage is the third of four stages of the Pleistocene Series. It corresponds to all rocks deposited during the Ionian Age (781,000 to 126,000 years ago) of the Pleistocene Epoch in the Quaternary Period. Although no established GSSP defining the base of the Ionian Stage has been formally established, three locations are under consideration. Two of these three candidate sections lie close to the Ionian Sea, the body of water after which this unit is named.

The first two GSSP candidate sections for this interval are located in southern Italy: Montalbano Jorica in the Basilicata region and Valle di Manche in the Calabria region. The third is located in Chiba, Japan. Presumably, the GSSP will be set into rock indicative of the base of the Brunhes-Matuyama paleomagnetic boundary.

TARANTIAN STAGE

The Tarantian Stage is the last of four stages of the Pleistocene Series, encompassing all rocks deposited during the Tarantian Age (126,000 to 11,700 years ago) of the

Pleistocene Epoch in the Quaternary Period. The name of this interval is derived from the European regional stage of the same name.

No GSSP defining the base of this unit has been formally established. A point located in a terminal borehole in the city of Amsterdam, Neth., was accepted by the ICS in 2008, but it has not been ratified by the IUGS. The point sits at the base of a rock layer that indicates the beginning of the Eemian interglacial stage (or the base of marine isotope stage 5e). No other indicators, biological or otherwise, currently mark the beginning of this interval. The Tarantian Stage overlies the Ionian Stage and underlies the Holocene Series.

PLEISTOCENE EVENTS AND ENVIRONMENTS

Environments during the Pleistocene were dynamic and underwent dramatic change in response to cycles of climatic change and the development of large ice sheets. Essentially, all regions of the Earth were influenced by these climatic events, but the magnitude and direction of environmental change varied from place to place. The best-known are those that occurred from the time of the last interglaciation, about 125,000 years ago, to the present.

GLACIATION

The growth of large ice sheets, ice caps, and long valley glaciers was among the most significant events of the Pleistocene. During times of extensive glaciation, more than 45 million square km (or about 30 percent) of the Earth's land area were covered by glaciers, and portions of the northern oceans were either frozen over or had extensive ice shelves. In addition to the Antarctic and Greenland ice sheets, most glacial ice was located in the Northern Hemisphere, where large ice sheets extended to mid-latitude regions. The largest was the Laurentide Ice Sheet in North America, which at times stretched from the Canadian Rocky Mountains on the west to Nova Scotia and Newfoundland on the east and from southern Illinois on the south to the Canadian Arctic on the north. The other major ice sheet in North America was the Cordilleran Ice Sheet, which formed in the mountainous region from western Alaska to northern Washington. Glaciers and ice caps were more widespread in other mountainous areas of the western United States, Mexico, Central America, and Alaska, as well as on the islands of Arctic Canada where an ice sheet has been postulated.

Although smaller in size, the Scandinavian Ice Sheet was similar to the Laurentide in character. At times, it covered most of Great Britain, where it incorporated several small British ice caps, and extended south across central Germany and Poland and then northeast across the northern Russian Plain to the Arctic Ocean. To the east in northern Siberia and on the Arctic Shelf of Eurasia, many small ice caps and domes developed in highland areas, and some of them may have coalesced to form ice sheets on the shallow shelf areas of the Arctic Ocean. Glaciers and small ice caps formed in the Alps and in the other high mountains of Europe and Asia. In the Southern Hemisphere, the Patagonia Ice Cap developed in the southern Andes, and ice caps and larger valley glaciers formed in the central and northern Andes. Glaciers also developed in New Zealand and on the higher mountains of Africa and Tasmania, including some located on the equator.

The results of glaciation varied greatly, depending on regional and local conditions. Glacial processes were concentrated near the base of the glacier and in the marginal zone. Material eroded at the base was transported toward the margin, where it was deposited both at the glacier bed and in the marginal area. These processes stripped large quantities of material from the central zones of the ice sheet and deposited it in the marginal zone and beyond the ice sheet. The Laurentide and Scandinavian ice sheets scoured and eroded bedrock terrain in their central areas, leaving behind many lakes and relatively thin glacial drift. Conversely, the Central Lowland and the northern Great Plains of the United States and the western plains of Canada, as well as northern Germany and Poland, southern Sweden, and portions of eastern and northern Russia, contain relatively thick deposits of till and other glacial sediment. The landscape of such areas is flat to gently rolling. Today, these areas are among the great agricultural regions of the world, which is in large part attributable to glaciation.

The effects in mountainous terrain were even more dramatic. Glacial processes were concentrated in the upper regions where snow accumulated and in the valleys through which the glaciers moved to lower elevations. These valley glaciers carved towering peaks (such as the Matterhorn in the Alps), large rock basins, and sweeping U-shaped valleys and left some of the most spectacular scenery on the Earth, with many high-level lakes and waterfalls. The lower portions of the valleys commonly contain ridges of glacial drift. Ridges of this sort that form along valley slopes are called lateral moraines, while those that loop across a valley at the lower end of a glacier are termed end moraines. The earliest observations and interpretations of more extensive Pleistocene glaciation were made on such deposits and landforms in the Alps during the early part of the 19th century.

The Matterhorn overlooking an Alpine valley. © Corbis

Periglacial Environments

The environment around the ice sheets was markedly different from that of today in these formerly glaciated areas. Temperatures were much lower, and a zone of permafrost (perennially frozen ground) developed around the southern margin of the ice sheets in both North America and Eurasia. This zone was relatively narrow in central North America, on the order of 200 km (124.274 miles), but in Europe and Russia it extended many hundreds of kilometres south of the ice margin. Mean annual temperatures near the ice margin were about -6°C (21°F) or colder and increased away from the ice margin to about 0°C (32°F) near the southern extent of the permafrost. Compared to present-day conditions, the mean air temperature was on the order of 12 to 20°C (22 to 36°F) colder near the ice margin. These conditions are indicated by ice-wedge casts and large-scale patterned ground, which are relict forms of ice wedges and tundra polygons that form today only in areas with continuous permafrost. Frost activity through freezing and thawing was intensified, and in areas of more relief talus accumulations and large block fields formed along escarpments and valley sides. Mass-wasting processes also were intensified and much material was eroded from slopes in periglacial areas. Deposits and landforms from such activity are known from the British Isles, northern Europe, and what was formerly the Soviet Union.

Lacustrine Environments

Large lakes, usually many times bigger than their modern counterparts, were common during the Pleistocene. They fluctuated in level in response to the major climatic cycles or the opening and closing of outlets due to glaciation and vertical movements of land areas. Some lakes were closely tied to glaciation. In North America a series of large pro-glacial lakes formed around the margin of the Laurentide Ice Sheet during backwasting (recession) of the ice margin into the Hudson Bay. The lakes were confined in part by the ice margin and in part by higher land to the south, east, and west. One of the largest was Lake Agassiz, which covered sizable areas of Manitoba, Ontario, and Saskatchewan and extended into North Dakota and Minnesota. The Great Lakes also formed as a result of glaciation as lobes of ice moved down preexisting lowlands and scoured out the weak rocks in the basins. Other lakes formed in the Champlain and Hudson valleys in eastern North America

The Great Lakes formed when tremendous glaciers scoured out weak rock in the basins, which gradually filled with water as the glaciers receded. Jeff Schmaltz, MODIS Rapid Response Team, NASA/GSFC

during deglaciation, and similar glacial lakes developed around the Scandinavian Ice Sheet and in other glaciated regions.

Of equal interest was the development of large lakes in areas that today have arid to semiarid climatic regimes and generally lack lakes or have modern lakes that are much reduced in size and are saline in character. Such lakes are referred to as pluvial lakes, and the climate under which they existed is termed a pluvial climate. Most of these lakes existed in closed basins that lacked outlets, and thus their levels were related to relative amounts of precipitation and evaporation. A record of fluctuating lake levels is provided by ancient shorelines and beach deposits that are present along the slopes of the enclosing mountains as well as by the sediment and soil record preserved in the subsurface deposits of the lake basins. The history of lake fluctuations varies somewhat locally within a region but may be much different from one region of the world to another, depending on the local and regional climate.

In the Great Basin of Utah, Nevada, California, and Oregon and in other areas of the western and southwestern United States and Mexico, about 100 basins contained lakes during the Pleistocene. The largest of these was Lake Bonneville, the predecessor of the modern Great Salt Lake in Utah. At its highest stage Lake Bonneville covered an area of about 52,000 square km (20,077 sq miles), and its maximum depth was approximately 370 metres (1,214 feet). These conditions existed about 15,000 years ago during the interval of the last major Pleistocene glaciation. Lake Bonneville shrank rapidly in size and, by 12,000 years ago, had permanently shrunk to a point where it had become smaller than the Great Salt Lake. A long record of fluctuating lake levels is evident from a 930-metre (3,051 feet) core taken in the Searles Lake basin in California. Parts of the sediment record from the core sample indicate a deep lake with lacustrine silts and clays and freshwater fossils. Other parts contain unusual evaporite minerals, which indicate that the lake was shallow and highly saline or even evidence of sediment exposure indicative of the complete desiccation of the lake. The inferred climatic record from the core is similar to the marine oxygen isotope record but differs in that it shows more variation in the amplitude of the climatic cycles.

Pluvial lakes in these areas were most extensive during times of widespread glaciation in the Northern Hemisphere and were low or dry during times of reduced glacial cover. Paleoclimatic modeling suggests that the Laurentide Ice Sheet forced the polar jet stream south of its present-day position during glaciation. This brought more moisture from the Pacific into the desert areas of the southwestern United States, causing greater precipitation as well as producing more cloud cover, which, together with lower temperatures, resulted in less evaporation.

Pluvial lakes also were common in other dry regions of the world, particularly in the subtropical zones, including eastern and northern Africa and portions of Australia, Asia, and the Middle East. Examples of these pluvial bodies are the Dead Sea in Jordan and Israel and Lake Chad in the southern Sahara. The latter, now a shallow saline lake, covered some 300,000 square km (115,830 sq miles) and was about six times the size of Lake Bonneville. Many lakes in the rift valleys of East Africa were larger and deeper than they are today. Among the better known and better understood are Lakes Rudolf, Victoria, Nakuru, Naivasha, Magadi, and Rukwa. Most of these lakes in the tropical and subtropical regions were not in phase with those in the Great Basin of North America. They were relatively high for some 20,000 or more years immediately before the last glaciation and again just after the last glaciation in the early Holocene. A long climatic record inferred from sediments in Lake George in southeastern Australia has characteristics similar to those of the marine oxygen isotope record. Alternating humid and arid climatic cycles were more rhythmic and of greater magnitude in the middle and late Pleistocene than earlier, and a major change in basin hydrology occurred approximately 2.5 million years ago.

FLUVIAL ENVIRONMENTS

Rivers and the valleys that they occupy were strongly affected by the changing climates of the Pleistocene. River channels and their sediment record are controlled in large part by the amount and type of load that is supplied by their drainage basins and the discharge or quantity of water available for flow. Both are closely related to climate, which not only includes precipitation, evaporation, and seasonality but also controls the extent of the vegetative cover of the land and the type and intensity of weathering processes. In addition, because of sea-level changes related to glaciation, the base level of rivers in coastal regions also fluctuated by significant amounts. As a result, river environments were dynamic and variable.

This was true for most rivers, but particularly so for rivers that drained large quantities of meltwater and sediment from the glacier margins. During glaciation, rivers of the latter kind developed braided-channel patterns in response to the input of large quantities of sediment derived from the melting glaciers and subglacial waters and to the large fluctuations in the quantity of water flowing at any one time, which varied because of seasonal and diurnal controls on the generation of meltwater. During times of glaciation, many of these rivers deposited thick sequences of sand and gravel in their valleys, such as those of the Hudson, Mississippi, and Ohio rivers in the United

States and of the Thames, Elbe, Rhine, and Seine rivers in Europe. Similar valleys have been buried by younger glacial deposits and are no longer evident at the surface. They exist today as bedrock valleys with thick fills of fluvial sand and gravel or lacustrine silt in localities where lakes existed in the valleys as a result of glacial damming. The sand and gravel fill in the surface valleys provide aggregate material for construction, and much groundwater is derived from the fills of both surface and buried valleys.

Some glacial valleys, as well as large upland areas, were sites of major catastrophic floods that resulted from the sudden drainage of proglacial and subglacial lakes. Such floods are known as *jökulhlaups*, an Icelandic term for subglacial lake outbursts. The largest and best-known floods of this type occurred in the Channeled Scabland of the Columbia Plateau region in eastern Washington State. Ice tongues flowing south from the Cordilleran Ice Sheet periodically dammed the Clark Fork River, forming glacial Lake Missoula. At times, Lake Missoula stretched more than 200 km (124 miles) upvalley and was about 600 metres (1,968 feet) deep near the ice dam. Sudden failure of the ice dam released more than 2,000 cubic km (480 cubic miles) of water, which flooded westward and southward across the Columbia Plateau and down the Columbia River valley. The floods cut through a loess cover into basalt and left a system of large dry channels with waterfalls, potholes, and longitudinal grooves in the basalt. Associated with the dry channels are huge, coarse gravel bars and giant current ripples. Other large catastrophic floods resulted from the sudden drainage of glacial Lake Agassiz and from the ancestral Great Lakes, as well as from some nonglacial lakes such as Lake Bonneville in the Great Basin. During the Anglian–Elsterian glaciation in Europe, a large ice-dammed lake formed in the North Sea, and large overflows from it initiated cutting of the Dover Straits.

During the transition from glacial to interglacial conditions, river channel patterns evolved from braided to meandering as a result of decreased load and possibly discharge. Near glaciated areas, rivers eroded into glacial outwash and left a system of stream terraces along the sides of most valleys. These modern interglacial rivers are much smaller than their glacial counterparts and are underfit (that is, appear too small) with respect to the large valleys in which they flow. In contrast, near coastal areas rivers actively built up their channels during the transition to interglacial conditions in response to rising sea level.

COASTAL ENVIRONMENTS AND SEA-LEVEL CHANGES

Coastal environments during the Pleistocene were controlled in large part by the fluctuating level of the sea as well as by local tectonic and environmental conditions. As a result of the many glaciations on land and the subsequent release of meltwater during interglacial times, sea level has fluctuated almost continuously between interglacial levels, like those of today, and levels during times of maximum glaciation, such as 18,000 years ago when sea level was more than 100 metres (300 feet) lower. At that time all the continental land areas were larger. Extensive areas of the world's continental shelves were exposed to weathering, soil formation, and fluvial and eolian activity and were inhabited by plants and animals. The Bering Shelf was exposed at this time and Siberia was connected to Alaska by a land bridge, thus allowing intercontinental migration of animals, including early humans. Rapid melting of the last large ice sheets resulted in a rising sea level that reached near modern level by the mid-Holocene, about 5,000 years ago. As a consequence, Pleistocene coastal environments are submerged below sea level in most parts of the world and are poorly known.

Fortunately, some coastal areas were undergoing tectonic uplift during the Pleistocene, so older shorelines and their deposits are exposed above modern sea level. Study of these deposits is important in understanding the recent sea-level record and in relating it to the record of glaciation. The most important are shorelines that contain coral reefs, because it is possible to obtain radiometric ages on fossils in the reef complex. Two of the most important and best-dated records are on the island of Barbados in the Caribbean and along the Huron Peninsula of New Guinea. The latter area exposes a spectacular suite of coastal terraces due to steady and rapid uplift during the Pleistocene. Age determinations of the terraces indicate times of relatively high sea level and suggest that they occurred at intervals of about 20,000 years. The highest sea level prior to the modern level occurred about 125,000 years ago and correlates with the peak warm interval of the last interglaciation (^{18}O stage 5e). Sea level at that time was about 6 metres (20 feet) higher than it is today.

EOLIAN ACTIVITY

Eolian deposits are important in the Pleistocene record and indicate widespread wind action at certain times and in certain areas. Mention has already been made of the importance of loess–paleosol records in working out regional chronologies and paleoclimatic history. Loess blankets large portions of the central and northwestern United States, Alaska, the east European plain of Russia, and southern Europe, where it is closely related to episodes of glaciation or to the cold periglacial climate beyond the ice-sheet margins or to both. The loess was derived primarily from the broad floodplains of the braided rivers draining meltwater and sediment away from the glaciers as well as from newly exposed glacial drift. Locally, sand dunes and sheets of sand occur near the valley sources and in some cases cover large upland areas, as in central and northern Europe. Convesely, the loess in China is considered to have been deflated mostly from such desert areas as the Gobi.

The deserts of the subtropical regions also experienced eolian activity during the Pleistocene. In Australia, the time of peak aridity and maximum dune activity (about 20,000 to 12,000 years ago) correlates with the time of peak glaciation in the Northern Hemisphere. This also was the case in the Sahara and other deserts in Africa, India, and the Middle East. One estimate is that the tropical arid zones were five times larger during times of peak glaciation. Sea level was lower at these times, the water was colder, and tropical cyclones were less extensive, resulting in decreased rainfall. These episodes of intensified eolian activity are recorded in other Pleistocene records. Ocean cores taken downwind of these regions contain windblown sediment in the portions of the core that accumulated during times of maximum eolian activity. In addition, microparticles occur in ice cores taken from the Greenland and Antarctic ice sheets and are concentrated at times of maximum glaciation and aridity in the subtropical deserts. At other times, the climate was less arid and the desert areas contracted, and vegetation developed to stabilize the dunes under more humid (pluvial) conditions.

Tectonic and Isostatic Movements

The lithospheric plates continued to shift during the Pleistocene, but the continents essentially were in their modern position at the start of the epoch. Of more importance to subsequent Quaternary events were the late Tertiary tectonic movements that affected the evolution of climate toward that of the Quaternary. Among these were the formation of the Isthmus of Panama, which affected oceanic circulation, and the uplift of the Tibetan Plateau and broad regional areas of the western United States, which affected atmospheric circulation, particularly the position and configuration of the polar jet stream.

Vertical movements of the Earth's crust also were caused by the formation and melting of large ice sheets. The area beneath an ice sheet subsides during glaciation because the crust is unable to sustain the weight of the glacier. These isostatic movements take place through the flow of material in the Earth's mantle, and the amount of subsidence amounts to about one-third the thickness of the ice sheet (for example, about 1 km [.6 mile] in the central area of the Laurentide Ice Sheet in Canada). Melting of the ice sheet removes the load and causes the ground to rise, or rebound. Such uplift is rapid at first but

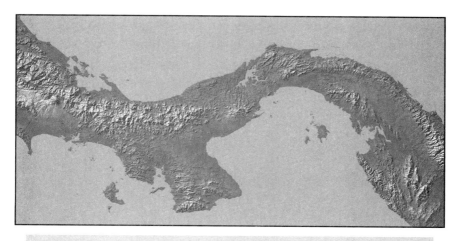

Crucial late Tertiary tectonic movements, the likes of which created the Isthmus of Panama, completely altered oceanic circulation and thus the climate. NASA

decreases with time. More than 300 metres (984 feet) of uplift has occurred in the eastern Hudson Bay area since that area was deglaciated. Substantial uplifting also took place prior to the complete melting of the ice sheets, and upward crustal movement continues today at a maximum rate of about 1.3 cm (.05 inch) per year. A similar record of glacio-isostatic adjustments is encountered in Fennoscandia, where the greatest depression and subsequent uplift related to the Scandinavian Ice Sheet is located in the Gulf of Bothnia.

PLEISTOCENE FAUNA AND FLORA

In many respects, the plants and animals of the Pleistocene are similar to those living today, but important differences exist. Moreover, the spatial distribution of various Pleistocene fauna and flora types differed markedly from what it is at present. Changes in climate and environment caused large-scale migrations of both plants and animals, evolutionary adaptations, and in some cases extinction. Study of the biota provides not only data on the past paleoenvironments but also insights into the response of plants and animals to well-documented environmental change. Of particular importance is the evolution of the genus *Homo* during the Pleistocene and the extinction of large mammals at the end of the epoch.

EVOLUTIONARY CHANGES

Evolutionary changes during the Pleistocene generally were minor because of the short interval of time involved. They were greatest among the mammals. In fact, the epoch has been subdivided into mammalian ages on the basis of the appearance of certain immigrant or endemic forms.

Mammalian evolution included the development of large forms, many of which became adapted to Arctic conditions. Among these were the woolly mammoth, woolly rhinoceros, musk ox, moose, reindeer, and others that inhabited the cold periglacial areas. Large mammals that inhabited the more temperate zones included the elephant, mastodon, bison, hippopotamus, wild hog, deer, giant beaver, horse, and ground sloth. The evolution of these as well as of much smaller forms was affected in part by three factors: (1) a generally cooler, more arid climate subject to periodic fluctuations, (2) new migration routes resulting largely from the emergence of intercontinental connections during times of lower sea level, and (3) a changing geography resulting from the uplift of plateaus and mountain building.

The most significant biological development was the appearance and evolution of the genus *Homo*. The oldest species, *H. habilis*, probably evolved from an australopithecine ancestor in the late Pliocene. The species was present in Africa by 2 million years ago and is known from sites as young as 1.5 million years old. Another extinct species, *H. erectus*, evolved in Africa, possibly from *H. habilis*, and is known from sites about 1.6 million years old. *H. erectus* spread to other parts of the Old World during the early Pleistocene and is known from northern China and Java by roughly 1 million years ago. Representatives of this group are known from many sites, and these beings constituted the dominant human species for more than a million years. The species *H. sapiens*, to which all modern humans belong, evolved in the later part of the middle Pleistocene, and early forms of the species are known from about 400,000 years ago. More modern forms of *H. sapiens*, the Neanderthals, appeared approximately 100,000 years ago during the last interglaciation and are known from many sites in Europe and western Asia. They disappeared about 35,000 to 30,000 years ago, and by then populations with fully modern skeletons had evolved and were widespread in the Old World.

Exactly when modern *H. sapiens* entered the New World remains controversial. It appears that fully evolved humans had migrated as far as Alaska from Siberia via the Bering land bridge by 30,000 years ago, and large numbers presumably moved south down the Canadian plains corridor between the Cordilleran and Laurentide ice sheets when it opened near the end of the last glaciation some 12,000 years ago. Conflicting and not fully accepted evidence at a few sites in the United States and in southern South America, however, suggests occupation of the continental interior prior to 30,000 years ago. If such findings are valid, the group of earlier immigrants may have arrived by small ocean-going craft from the Pacific Islands.

THE MIGRATION OF PLANTS AND ANIMALS

Changing environments in response to climatic variation caused drastic disruptions of faunas and floras both on land and in the oceans. These disruptions were greatest near the former ice sheets that extended far to the south and caused the southward displacement of climatic and vegetation zones. In the temperate zones of central Europe and the United States where deciduous forests exist today, vegetation was open and most closely resembled the northern tundra, with grasses, herbs, and few trees during glacial intervals. Farther south, a broad region of boreal forests with varying proportions of spruce and pine or a combination of both extended almost to the Mediterranean in Europe and northern Louisiana in North America. The vegetation succession has been documented by studies of fossil pollen, which accumulated year by year with other sediments in lakes and bogs beyond the ice margin.

Although such floral migrations appear simple in concept, interpretation of the vegetation record is quite complicated, because many glacial pollen assemblages have no modern analogues. Similar relationships also occur with vertebrate faunas: more temperate forms commonly occur together with more Arctic forms. Such "disharmonious" faunas suggest that glacial climatic and environmental conditions in some cases were totally unlike those of any modern environment. One explanation is that climatic conditions may have been more equable during glacial times and may have lacked the seasonal extremes of modern climates in such areas. Although overall temperatures were significantly lower, summers probably were much cooler because of the influence of the ice sheet, and winters, except very near the ice margin, lacked severe cold spells, as the ice sheet formed a barrier to Arctic air masses that today bring freezing conditions far to the south. Thus, plants and animals whose geographic ranges would ordinarily be controlled by either extreme seasonal warm or cold conditions could coexist during glacial times, and considerable community reorganization took place in response to climatic change during and following a glaciation.

Similar responses to changing environments are well known from life in the oceans. Marine organisms closely reflect the temperature, depth, and salinity of the water in which they live, and studies of the fossil succession from deep-sea cores have allowed detailed reconstructions of oceanic conditions for the late Pleistocene. Planktonic foraminifers are most useful for determining sea-surface conditions, and changes in the distribution of polar, subpolar, subtropical, and tropical faunas have been used to map changing oceanic conditions. Changes in the North Atlantic Ocean were most dramatic because of the direct influence of the ice sheets to the west, north, and east.

During episodes of glaciation, polar faunas extended south to about 45° N latitude, whereas during interglaciations these faunas occurred mostly north of 70° and subtropical faunas extended far to the north under the influence of the Gulf Stream.

MEGAFAUNAL EXTINCTIONS

The end of the Pleistocene was marked by the extinction of many genera of large mammals, including mammoths, mastodons, ground sloths, and giant beavers. The extinction event is most distinct in North America, where 32 genera of large mammals vanished during an interval of about 2,000 years, centred on 11,000 BP. On other continents, fewer genera disappeared, and the extinctions were spread over a somewhat longer time span. Nonetheless, they still appear to be more common near the end of the Pleistocene than at any other time during the epoch. Except on islands, small mammals, along with reptiles and amphibians, generally were not affected by the extinction process. The cause of the extinctions has been vigorously debated, with two main hypotheses being advanced: (1) the extinctions were the result of overpredation by human hunters; and (2) they were the result of abrupt climatic and vegetation changes during the last glacial–interglacial transition.

The first theory, the so-called overkill hypothesis, receives support from the coincidence in the timing of the mass extinction and the appearance of large numbers of human hunters, as evidenced by the Clovis complex, an ancient culture centred in North America. Clovis archaeological sites (concentrated in Arizona, New Mexico, and West Texas), with their distinctive projectile points, date between 10,000 and 12,000 years ago. Proponents of the hypothesis point out that these new immigrants from

Eurasia were skilled hunters; the North American fauna would not have been wary of this new group of predators; and, once the number of large herbivores declined, large carnivores also would have been affected as their prey became extinct. In addition to direct slaughter, human disruption of the environment most likely contributed to the extinctions, particularly on other continents.

Abrupt climatic change also occurred at the time of the megafaunal extinctions, and so timing alone does not clearly differentiate one hypothesis from the other. The climatic-change hypothesis takes a number of forms but essentially focuses on the reorganization of vegetation, availability of food (including nutrient value), and general environmental disruption and stress that resulted as climates became more seasonal. It appears likely that the causes of extinction varied in different geographic areas under different conditions and that both climatic change and human activities played roles but of varying importance in different situations.

CAUSE OF THE CLIMATIC CHANGES AND GLACIATIONS

Pleistocene climates and the cause of the climatic cycles that resulted in the development of large-scale continental ice sheets have been a topic of study and debate for more than 100 years. Many theories have been proposed to account for Quaternary glaciations, but most are deficient in view of current scientific knowledge about Pleistocene climates. One early theory, the theory of astronomical cycles, seems to explain much of the climatic record and is considered by most to best account for the fundamental cause or driving force of the climatic cycles.

The astronomical theory is based on the geometry of the Earth's orbit around the Sun, which affects how solar radiation is distributed over the surface of the planet. The latter is determined by three orbital parameters that have cyclic frequencies: (1) the eccentricity of the Earth's orbit (that is, its departure from a circular orbit), with a frequency of about 100,000 years; (2) the obliquity, or tilt, of the Earth's axis away from a vertical drawn to the plane of the planet's orbit, with a frequency of 41,000 years; and (3) the precession, or wobble, of the Earth's axis, with frequencies of 19,000 and 23,000 years. Collectively, these parameters determine the amount of radiation received at any latitude during any season. Radiation curves have been calculated from them for different latitudes for the past 600,000 years. These curves vary systematically from the poles to the equator, with those in the higher latitudes being dominated by the 41,000-year tilt cycle and those in lower latitudes by the 19,000- and 23,000-year precession cycles. The astronomical theory places emphasis on summer insolation in the high-latitude areas of the Northern Hemisphere (about 55° N latitude). Glaciations are hypothesized to begin during times of low summer insolation when conditions should be most optimal for winter snow to last through the summer season.

Dating of the marine terraces in Barbados and New Guinea and, more importantly, determining the chronology of glaciations as inferred from the marine oxygen isotope record were milestones in testing the astronomical theory. Early spectral analysis of the oxygen isotope record of cores from the deep ocean showed frequencies of climatic variation at essentially the same frequencies as the orbital cycles (that is to say, at 100,000 years, 43,000 years, 24,000 years, and 19,000 years). These results (reported in 1976), along with those of more recent analyses, provide firm evidence of a tie between orbital cycles and the Earth's recent climatic record. The variations in the Earth's orbit are generally considered the "pacemaker" of the ice ages.

Although the planetary orbital cycles are the likely cause of the Pleistocene climatic cycles, the mechanisms and connections to the global climate are not fully understood, and important questions remain unanswered. The relatively small seasonal and latitudinal radiation variations alone cannot account for the magnitude of climatic change as experienced by the Earth during the Pleistocene. Clearly, feedback mechanisms must operate to amplify the insolation changes caused by the orbital parameters. One of these is albedo, the reflectivity of the Earth's surface. Increased snow cover in high-latitude areas would cause increased cooling. Another feedback mechanism is the decreased carbon dioxide content of the atmosphere during times of glaciation, as recorded in the bubbles of long ice cores. Variations in atmospheric carbon dioxide are essentially synchronous with global climatic change and thus in all likelihood played a significant role through the so-called greenhouse effect. (The latter phenomenon refers to the trapping of heat, or infrared radiation, in the lower levels of the atmosphere by carbon dioxide, water vapour, and certain other gases.) Another atmospheric effect is the increased amount of dust during glacial times, as borne out by ice core and loess records. All these changes operate in the same direction, causing increased cooling during glacial times and warming during interglacial times.

Other problems remain with respect to the astronomical theory. One is the dominance of the 100,000-year cycle in the Pleistocene climatic record, whereas the eccentricity cycle is the weakest among the orbital parameters. Another is the cause of the asymmetrical pattern of the climatic record. Ice ages appear to start slowly and take a long time to build up to maximum glaciation, only to terminate abruptly and go from maximum glacial to full interglacial conditions in less than 10,000 years. A third problem is the synchronous nature of the climatic record between the Northern and Southern hemispheres, which one would not expect from the orbital parameters because they operate in different directions in the two hemispheres.

Different approaches have been taken to explain these questions, but most suggest that the Northern Hemisphere with its enormous continental ice sheets was the controlling area and that the ice sheets themselves with their complex dynamics may explain the 100,000-year climatic cycle. Others propose that major reorganizations of the ocean–atmosphere system must be called upon to explain the climatic record. These reorganizations are concerned with the transport of salt through the oceans and water vapour through the atmosphere and revolve around the existence and strength of deep oceanic currents in the Atlantic Ocean.

Ongoing interdisciplinary research on Pleistocene paleoclimatology is focused on understanding the complex dynamics and interactions among the atmosphere, oceans, and ice sheets. Such research is expected to provide further insight into the cause of the climatic cycles, which is essential as scientists attempt to predict future climates in view of recent human-induced modifications of the climatic system.

CHAPTER 7

THE HOLOCENE EPOCH

The Holocene, which was formerly known as the Recent Epoch, is the younger of the two epochs that constitute the Quaternary Period and the latest interval of geologic time, covering approximately the last 11,700 years of the Earth's history. The sediments of the Holocene, both continental and marine, cover the largest area of the globe of any epoch in the geologic record, but the Holocene is unique because it is coincident with the late and post-Stone Age history of mankind. The influence of humans is of world extent and is so profound that it seems appropriate to have a special geologic name for this time.

In 1833 Charles Lyell proposed the designation Recent for the period that has elapsed since "the earth has been tenanted by man." It is now known that humans have been in existence a great deal longer. The term Holocene was proposed in 1867 and was formally submitted to the International Geological Congress at Bologna, Italy, in 1885. It was officially endorsed by the U.S. Commission on Stratigraphic Nomenclature in 1969.

The Holocene represents the most recent interglacial interval of the Quaternary period. The preceding and substantially longer sequence of alternating glacial and interglacial ages is the Pleistocene Epoch. Because there is nothing to suggest that the Pleistocene has actually ended, certain authorities prefer to extend the Pleistocene up to the present time, but this approach tends to ignore humans and their effect. The Holocene forms the chronological framework for human history. Archaeologists use it

Geologist Charles Lyell helped set the foundation for understanding of Earth's development. Hulton Archive/Getty Images

as the time standard against which they trace the development of early civilizations.

HOLOCENE STRATIGRAPHY

The Holocene is unique among geologic epochs because varied means of correlating deposits and establishing chronologies are available. One of the most important means is carbon-14 dating. Because the age determined by the carbon-14 method may be appreciably different from the true age in certain cases, it is customary to refer to such dates in "radiocarbon years." These dates, obtained from a variety of deposits, form an important framework for Holocene stratigraphy and chronology.

CHRONOLOGY AND CORRELATION

The limitations of accuracy of radiocarbon age determinations are expressed as ± a few tens or hundreds of years. In addition to this calculated error, there also is a question of error caused by contamination of the material measured. For instance, an ancient peat may contain some younger roots and thus give a falsely "young" age unless it is carefully collected and treated to remove contaminants. Marine shells consist of calcium carbonate ($CaCO_3$), and in certain coastal regions there is upwelling of deep oceanic water that can be 500 to more than 1,000 years old. An "age" from living shells in such an area can suggest that they are already hundreds of years old.

In certain areas a varve chronology can be established. This involves counting and measuring thicknesses in annual paired layers of lake sediments deposited in lakes that undergo an annual freeze-up. Because each year's sediment accumulation varies in thickness according to the climatic conditions of the melt season, any long sequence of varve measurements provides a distinctive "signature" and can be correlated for moderate distances from lake basin to lake basin. The pioneer in this work was the Swedish investigator Baron Gerard De Geer.

In some relatively recent continental deposits, obsidian (a black glassy rock of volcanic origin) can be used for dating. Obsidian weathers slowly at a uniform rate, and the thickness of the weathered layer is measured microscopically and gauged against known standards to give a date in years. This has been particularly useful where arrowheads of obsidian are included in deposits.

Paleomagnetism is another phenomenon used in chronology. The Earth's magnetic field undergoes a secular shift that is fairly well known for the last 2,000 years. The magnetized material to be studied can be natural, such as a lava flow; or it may be man-made, as, for example, an ancient brick kiln or smeltery that has cooled and thus fixed the magnetic orientation of the bricks to correspond to the geomagnetic field of that time.

Another form of dating is tephrochronology, so called because it employs the tephra (ash layers) generated by volcanic eruptions. The wind may blow the ash 1,500–3,000 km (932-1,864 miles), and, because the minerals or volcanic glass from any one eruptive cycle tend to be distinctive from those of any other cycle, even from the same volcano, these can be dated from the associated lavas by stratigraphic methods (with or without absolute dating). The ash layer then can be traced as a "time horizon" wherever it has been preserved. When the Mount Mazama volcano in Oregon exploded at about 6600 BP (radiocarbon-dated by burned wood), 70 cubic km (17 cubic miles) of debris were thrown into the air, forming the basin now occupied by Crater Lake. The tephra were distributed over 10 states, thereby providing a chronological marker horizon. A comparable eruption of Thera on Santorin in the Aegean Sea about 3,400 years ago left tephra in the deep-sea sediments and on adjacent land areas. Periodic eruptions of Mount Hekla in Iceland have been of use in Scandinavia, which lies downwind.

Finally, the measurement and analysis of tree rings (or dendrochronology) must be mentioned. The age of a tree that has grown in any region with a seasonal contrast in climate can be established by counting its growth rings. Work in this field by the University of Arizona's Laboratory of Tree-Ring Research, by selection of both living trees and deadwood, has carried the year-by-year chronology back more than 7,500 years. Certain pitfalls have been discovered in tree-ring analysis, however. Sometimes, such as in a severe season, a growth ring may not form. In certain latitudes the tree's ring growth correlates with moisture, but in others it may be correlated with temperature. From the climatic viewpoint these two parameters are often inversely related in different regions. Nevertheless, in experienced hands, just as with varve counting from adjacent lakes, ring measurements from trees with overlapping ages can extend chronologies back for many thousands of years. The bristlecone pine of California's White Mountains has proved to be singularly long-lived and suitable for this chronology. Some trees still living are more than 4,000 years old, certainly the oldest living organisms. Wood from old buildings and even old paving blocks in western Europe and in Russia have contributed to the chronology. This technique not only offers an additional means of dating but also contains a built-in documentation of climatic characteristics. In certain favourable situations, particularly in the drier, low latitudes, tree-ring records sometimes document 11- and 22-year sunspot cycles.

THE PLEISTOCENE–HOLOCENE BOUNDARY

Arguments can be presented for the selection of the lower boundary of the Holocene at several different times in the past. Some Russian investigators have proposed a boundary at the beginning of the Allerød, a warm interstadial age that began about 12,000 BP. Others, in Alaska, proposed a Holocene section beginning at 6000 BP. Marine geologists have recognized a worldwide change in the character of deep-sea sedimentation about 10,000–11,000 BP. In warm tropical waters, the clays show a sharp change at this time from chlorite-rich particles often associated with fresh feldspar grains (cold, dry climate indicators) to kaolinite and gibbsite (warm, wet climate indicators).

Some of the best-preserved traces of the boundary are found in southern Scandinavia, where the transition from the latest glacial stage of the Pleistocene to the Holocene was accompanied by a marine transgression. These beds, south of Göteborg, have been uplifted and are exposed at the surface. The boundary is dated around 10,300 ± 200 years BP (in radiocarbon years). This boundary marks the very beginning of warmer climates that occurred after the latest minor glacial advance in Scandinavia. This advance built the last Salpausselkä moraine, which corresponds in part to the Valders substage in North America. The subsequent warming trend was marked by the Finiglacial retreat in northern Scandinavia, the Ostendian (early Flandrian) marine transgression in northwestern Europe.

THE NATURE OF THE HOLOCENE RECORD

The very youthfulness of the Holocene stratigraphic sequence makes subdivision difficult. The relative slowness of the Earth's crustal movements means that most areas containing a complete marine stratigraphic sequence are still submerged. Fortunately, in areas that were depressed by the load of glacial ice, there has been progressive postglacial uplift (crustal rebound) that has led to the exposure of the nearshore deposits.

Deep Oceanic Deposits

The marine realm, apart from covering about 70 percent of the Earth's surface, offers far better opportunities than coastal environments for undisturbed preservation of sediments. In deep-sea cores, the boundary usually can be seen at a depth of about 10–30 cm (3.9–11.8 inches), where the Holocene sediments pass downward into material belonging to the late glacial stage of the Pleistocene. The boundary often is marked by a slight change in colour. For example, globigerina ooze, common in the ocean at intermediate depths, is frequently slightly pinkish when it is of Holocene age because of a trace of iron oxides that are characteristic of tropical soils. At greater depth in the section, the globigerina ooze may be grayish because of greater quantities of clay, chlorite, and feldspar that have been introduced from the erosion of semiarid hinterlands during glacial time.

During each glacial epoch the cooling ocean waters led to reduced evaporation and thus fewer clouds, then to lower rainfall, then to reduction of vegetation, and so eventually to the production of relatively more clastic sediments (owing to reduced chemical weathering). Furthermore, the worldwide eustatic (glacially related) lowering of sea level caused an acceleration of erosion along the lower courses of all rivers and on exposed continental shelves, so that clastic sedimentation rates in the oceans were higher during glacial stages than during the Holocene. Turbidity currents, generated on a large scale during the low sea-level periods, became much less frequent following the rise of sea level in the Holocene.

Studies of the fossils in the globigerina oozes show that at a depth in the cores that has been radiocarbon-dated at about 10,000–11,000 BP, the relative number of warm-water planktonic foraminiferans markedly increases. In addition, certain foraminiferal species tend to change their coiling direction from a left-handed spiral to a right-handed spiral at this time. This is attributed to the change from cool water to warm water, an extraordinary (and still not understood) physiological reaction to environmental stress. Many foraminiferans, however, responded to the warming water of the Holocene by migrating poleward by distances of as much as 1,000 to 3,000 km (621–1,684 miles) to remain within their optimal temperature habitats.

In addition to foraminiferans in the globigerina oozes, there are nannoplankton, minute fauna and flora consisting mainly of coccolithophores. Research on the present coccolith distribution shows that there is maximum productivity in zones of oceanic upwelling, notably at the subpolar convergence and the equatorial divergence. During the latest glacial stage, the subpolar zone was displaced toward the equator, but with the subsequent warming waters, it shifted back to the borders of the polar regions.

The distribution of the carbonate plankton bears on the problem of rates of oceanic circulation. Is the Holocene rate higher or lower than during the last glacial stage? It has been argued that, because of the higher mean temperature gradient in the lower atmosphere from equator to poles during the last glacial period, there would have been higher wind velocities and, because of the atmosphere–ocean coupling, higher oceanic current velocities. There were, however, two retarding factors for glacial-age currents. First, the eustatic withdrawal of oceanic waters from the continental shelves reduced the effective area of the oceans by 8 percent. Second, the greater extent of floating sea ice would have further reduced the available air–ocean coupling surface, especially in the critical zone of the westerly circulation. According to climatic studies by the British meteorologist Hubert H. Lamb, the presence of large continental ice sheets in North America and Eurasia would have introduced a strong blocking action to the normal zonal circulation of the atmosphere, which then would be replaced by more meridional circulation. This in turn would have been appreciably less effective in driving major oceanic current gyres.

CONTINENTAL SHELF AND COASTAL REGIONS

It was recognized as early as 1842 that a logical consequence of a glacial age would be a large-scale withdrawal of ocean water. Consequently, deglaciation would produce a postglacial "glacioeustatic" transgression of the seas across the continental shelf. The trace of this Holocene rise of sea level was first discerned along the New England coast and along the coast of Belgium, where it was named the Flandrian Transgression by Georges Dubois in 1924.

The deep-sea Holocene sediments usually follow without interruption upon those of the Upper Pleistocene, whereas on the continental shelf there is almost invariably a break in the sequence on the continental formations there. As sea level rose, it paused or fluctuated at various stages, leaving erosional terraces, beach deposits, and other indicators of the stillstand. Brief regressions in particular permitted the growth of peat deposits that are of significance in the Holocene record because they can be dated by radiocarbon analysis. Dredging in certain places on the shelf, such as off eastern North America, also is useful because terrestrial fossils from the latest glacial period or early Holocene have been found, ranging from mammoth and mastodon bones and tusks to human artifacts. On approximately 70 percent of the world's continental shelves today, the amount of sedimentary accumulation since the beginning of the Holocene is minimal, so that dredging or coring operations often disclose hard rock, with older formations at or close to the surface. In other places, especially near the former continental ice fronts, the shelf is covered by periglacial fluvial sands (meltwater deposits), which, because of their unconsolidated nature, became extensively reworked into beaches and bars during the Holocene Transgression.

In warm coral seas the major pauses in the Holocene eustatic rise were long enough for fringing reefs to become established. When the rise resumed, the reefs grew upward, either in ribbonlike barriers or from former headlands as patch reefs or shelf atolls. Because coral generally does not colonize a sediment-covered shelf floor at depths of more than about 10 metres (30 feet), those reefs now rising from greater depths must have been emplaced in the early Holocene or grown on foundations of ancient reefs.

The great ice-covered areas of the Quaternary Period included Antarctica, North America, Greenland, and Eurasia. Of these, Antarctica and Greenland have relatively high latitude situations and do not easily become deglaciated. Some melting occurs, but there is a great melt-retardation factor in high-latitude ice sheets (high albedo or reflectivity, short melt season, and so forth). In the case of mid-latitude ice sheets, however, once melting starts, the ice disappears at a tremendous rate. The melt rate reached a maximum about 8000 BP, liberating 18 trillion (18×10^{12}) metric tons of meltwater annually. This corresponds to a rise in sea level of 5 cm (2 inches) per year. Hand in hand with melting, the sea level responded so that, as the ice began to retreat from its former terminal moraines, the sea began to invade the former coastlands.

As the sea level rose, the Earth's crust responded buoyantly to the removal of the load of ice, and at critical times the rate of rise of the water level was outstripped by the rate of rise of the land. In these places the highest ancient shoreline that is now preserved is known as the marine limit. The nearer the former centre of the ice sheet, the higher the marine limit. In northern Scandinavia, Ontario and northwestern Quebec, around Hudson Bay, and in Baffin Island, it reaches more than a 300-metre (1,000-foot) elevation. In central Maine and Spitsbergen it may exceed 100 metres (300 feet), whereas in coastal Scotland and Northern Ireland it is rarely above 10–15 metres (30–50 feet).

In addition to the marine-limit strandlines, there are row upon row of lower beach levels stretched out across Scandinavia, around Hudson Bay, and on other Arctic coasts. These strandlines are dated and distinctive and do not grade into each other. Each represents a specific period of time when the rising crust and rising sea level remained in place long enough to permit the formation of beaches, spits, and bars and sometimes the erosion of headlands ("fossil cliffs").

A complicating factor near the periphery of former ice sheets is the so-called marginal bulge. Reginald A. Daly, an American geologist, postulated that, if the ice load pressed down the middle of the glaciated area, the Earth's crust in the marginal area tended to rise up slightly, producing a marginal bulge. With deglaciation the marginal bulge should slowly collapse. A fulcrum should develop between postglacial uplift and peripheral subsidence. In North America that fulcrum seems to run across Illinois to central New Jersey and then to swing northeastward, paralleling the coast and turning seaward north of Boston. In the Scandinavian region the fulcrum crosses central Denmark to swing around the Baltic Sea and then trends northeastward across the Gulf of Finland north of St. Petersburg, so that the southeastern Baltic and north-western Germany are subsiding. The Netherlands area is subsiding also, but here the pattern is complicated by the long-term negative tectonic trend of the North Sea Basin and the Rhine delta.

It seems likely that this fulcrum shifted inward toward the former glacial centre during the early part of the Holocene. Passing inland, the lines of equal uplift (iso-bases) are positive, whereas seaward they are negative.

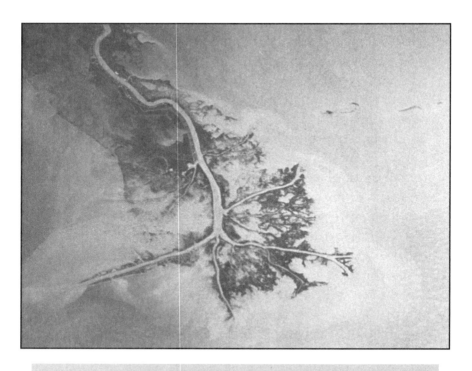

Deltas such as the Mississippi correspond with regions of tectonic subsid-ence and manifest unique Holocene sequences. StockTrek/Photodisc/ Getty Images

The coastal area of southern New England is still slowly subsiding at the present time (1–3 mm per year).

The great deltas of the world, those of the Mississippi, Rhine, Rhône, Danube, Nile, Amazon, Niger, Tigris-Euphrates, Ganges, and Indus, all coincide with regions of tectonic subsidence. Because water-saturated sediment has a tendency to compact under further sediment loading, there is an additional built-in mechanism that adds to the subsidence in such areas.

In this deltaic setting, Holocene sequences are found that are quite different from those in the postglacial uplifted regions. Whereas the Holocene beaches in the uplift areas extend horizontally across the country in concentric belts, the Holocene sequence in the deltaic regions is predominantly vertical in nature and can be studied only from well data.

In both the Mississippi and Rhine deltas, sediments that represent the earliest marine Holocene are missing. The sediments must lie seaward on the shelf margin, and the oldest marine layers are found to rest directly upon the late Pleistocene river silts and gravels. In a delta settling at about 0.5 to 3 mm (.01–.11 inch) per year, the rising sea of the Flandrian Transgression extended quickly across the river deposits to the inner margin (where there is a fulcrum comparable to that of the glaciated regions), marking the boundary between areas of downwarp and those of relative stability or gentle upwarp. The marine beds alternate with continental deposits that represent river or swamp environments. Six major fluctuations are recognizable in both the Mississippi and Rhine deltas. By radiocarbon dating the transgressive and regressive phases have been shown to be correlative in time.

On a subsiding coast there tends to be an alternation in importance between two types of associated sedimentary facies. During a regression of the sea the river distributaries are rejuvenated and there is an increase in the supply of sand and silt. Beaches widen and beach ridge dunes or cheniers may be formed. During a transgressive stage, the saltwater wedge at river mouths causes a back-up, and the estuary becomes much more sluggish (thalassostatic).

In the Netherlands the basal Holocene is buried in the fluvial deposits of the lower Rhine. The postglacial eustatic rise had to traverse the North Sea Plain and advance up the English Channel several hundred kilometres before it reached the Netherlands area. At about 9000–8500 BP (Ancylus stage in the Baltic), the coastal beaches still lay seaward from the present shore. Subsequently, they became stabilized by a brief eustatic regression, while the high water table permitted the growth of the Lower Peat. This is contemporaneous with the late Boreal Peat that is widespread in northern Europe, as well as Peat #5 of the Mississippi delta.

A further eustatic rise (of about 10–12 metres [32.8–39.3 feet]) ensued about 7750 BP, corresponding to a warming of the climate marked by the growth of oak forests in western Europe (the BAT, or "Boreal–Atlantic Transition"). In The Netherlands the barrier beaches re-formed close to the present coastline, and widespread tidal flats developed to the interior. These are known as the Calais Beds (or Calaisian) from the definition in Flanders by Dubois. In the protected inner margins, the peat continued to accumulate during and after the "Atlantic" time.

From evidence outside the areas of subsidence, it seems likely that the worldwide eustatic sea level rise reached its maximum sometime between 5500 and 2500 bp (many consider the date to be about 2000 BP). In The Netherlands, in spite of subsidence, the western coastline became more or less stabilized about 4000 BP with the beginning of the formation of the Older Dunes alternating with interdune soils. At the same time, in the tide flat areas the Calaisian was followed by the Dunkirk stage, or Dunkerquian.

The Younger Dune sequence of the Netherlands began with a dry climatic phase in the 12th century CE. With several fluctuations of cold continental climates, dune building continued until the 16th century. Only brief positive oscillations of sea level occurred until the 17th century, when the "modern" warming and eustatic rise started, accompanied also by dune stabilization.

Broadly comparable patterns occur in other areas, from France and Britain to Texas, Oregon, and Brazil. There is normally a threefold or fourfold subdivision in all the Holocene coastal dune belts, each extensively vegetated and consolidated before the successively younger dune belt was added. In many cases there is evidence from buried beach deposits that the foundations of the inner dunes are older strandlines that were established when the sea was somewhat higher than today. An important regressive phase seems to have initiated each new dune belt.

OTHER COASTAL REGIONS

Besides regions of glacio-isostatic crustal adjustment, both positive and negative, and the deltaic or geosynclinally subsiding areas, there are many tens of thousands of kilometres of coastlines that are relatively stable and a smaller fraction that are tectonically active.

Most striking scenically are the coasts with Holocene terraces undergoing tectonic uplift. Terraces of this sort, backed in successive steps by Pleistocene terraces, are well developed in South America, the East Indies, New Guinea, and Japan. By careful surveys every few years, Japanese geodesists have established mean rates of crustal uplift (or subsidence) for many parts of the country and have constructed a residual eustatic curve that is comparable with those obtained elsewhere.

Besides uplifted coasts outside of glaciated areas, there are also certain highly indented coasts that show clear evidence of Holocene "drowning." Typically, these coasts are characterized by the rias, or drowned estuaries, sculptured by fluvial action, but many of the valleys were cut 10 to 20 million years ago, and the Holocene history has been purely one of eustatic rise.

On the basis of the known climatic history of the Holocene, from the strandline record of Scandinavia and from the sedimentologic evolution of the Mississippi and Rhine deltas, an approximate chronology of Holocene eustasy can be worked out. The amplitudes of the fluctuations and the finite curve are less easily established. A first approximation of the oscillations was published in 1959 and in a more detailed way in 1961 (the so-called Fairbridge curve). Smoothed versions have been offered by several other workers.

HOLOCENE ENVIRONMENT AND BIOTA

In formerly glaciated regions, the Holocene has been a time for the reinstitution of ordinary processes of subaerial erosion and progressive reoccupation by a flora and fauna. The latter expanded rapidly into what was an ecological vacuum, but with a restricted range of organisms, because the climates were initially cold and the soil was still immature.

FLORAL CHANGE

The most important biological means of establishing Holocene climate involves palynology, the study of pollen, spores, and other microscopic organic particles. Pollen from trees, shrubs, or grasses is generated annually in large quantities and often is well preserved in fine-grained lake, swamp, or marine sediments. Statistical correlations of modern and fossil assemblages provide a basis for estimating the approximate makeup of the local or regional vegetation through time. Even a crude subdivision into arboreal pollen (AP) and nonarboreal pollen (NAP) reflects the former types of climate. The tundra vegetation of the last glacial epoch, for example, provides predominantly NAP, and the transition to forest vegetation shows the climatic amelioration that heralded the beginning of the Holocene.

The first standard palynological stratigraphy was developed in Scandinavia by Axel Blytt, Johan Rutger Sernander, and E.J. Lennart von Post, in combination with a theory of Holocene climate changes. The so-called Blytt–Sernander system was soon tied to the archaeology and to the varve chronology of Gerard De Geer. It has been closely checked by radiocarbon dating, establishing a useful standard. Every region has its own standard pollen stratigraphy, but these are now correlated approximately with the Blytt–Sernander framework. To some extent this is even true for remote areas such as Patagonia and East Africa. Particularly important is the fact that the middle Holocene was appreciably warmer than today. In Europe this phase has been called the Climatic Optimum (zones Boreal to Atlantic), and in North America it has been called the hypsithermal (also altithermal and xerothermic).

Like pollen, macrobotanical remains by themselves do not establish chronologies, but absolute dating of these remains provides a chronology of floral changes throughout the Holocene. Recent discoveries of the dung deposits of Pleistocene animals in dry caves and alcoves on the

Colorado Plateau, including those of mammoth, bison, horse, sloth, extinct forms of mountain goats, and shrub oxen, have provided floristic assemblages from which temperature and moisture requirements for such assemblages can be deduced to develop paleoenvironmental reconstructions tied to an absolute chronology. Macrobotanical remains found in the digestive tracts of late Pleistocene animals frozen in the permafrost regions of Siberia and Alaska also have made it possible to build paleoenvironmental reconstructions tied to absolute chronologies.

From these reconstructions, one can see warming and drying trends in the terminal Pleistocene (± 11,500 BP). Cold-tolerant, water-loving plants (such as birch and spruce) retreated to higher elevations or higher latitudes (as much as 2,500 metres [8,202 feet] in elevation) within less than 11,000 years.

Detailed studies of late Pleistocene and Holocene alluvium, tied to carbon-14 chronology, have provided evidence of cyclic fluctuations in the aggradation and degradation of Holocene drainage systems. Although it is still too early in the analysis to state with certainty, it appears from the work of several investigators that there is a regional, or semicontinental cycle, of erosion and deposition that occurs every 250–300, 500–600, 1,000–1,300, and possibly 6,000 years within the Holocene.

FAUNAL CHANGE

According to an analysis of multiple carbon-dated sites conducted in 1984 by James I. Mead and David J. Meltzer, 75 percent of the larger animals (those of more than 40 kilograms [90 pounds] live weight) that became extinct during the late Pleistocene did so by about 10,800 to 10,000 years ago. Whether the cause of this decimation of Pleistocene fauna was climatic or cultural has been debated ever since another American investigator, Paul S. Martin, proposed the overkill hypothesis in the 1960s. Since then, other hypotheses for the late Pleistocene extinctions, such as those involving climatic changes or disease outbreaks, have emerged. Whatever the case, most geologists and paleontologists designate the beginning of a new epoch—the Holocene—at approximately 11,700 years ago, a time coincident with the sudden ending of the Younger Dryas cool phase.

Floral and faunal reconstructions tied to the physical evidence of fluvial, alluvial, and lacustrine sediments and to a radiocarbon chronology reflect a warming and drying trend (as contrasted with the Pleistocene) during the last 10,000 years. The drying trend apparently reached its peak about 5,500 to 7,500 years ago (referred to as Antev's Altithermal) and has ranged between that peak and the cold, wet conditions of the early Holocene since that time.

Nonmarine Holocene sediments are usually discontinuous, making exact correlations difficult. An absolute chronology provided by radiocarbon dating permits temporal correlation, even if the deposits are discontinuous or physically different. Analysis of Holocene deposits requires chronostratigraphic correlations of discontinuous and dissimilar deposits to allow an interpretation of local, regional, continental, and global conditions.

Analysis of microfauna from paleontological and archaeological sites of the late Pleistocene and Holocene of North America has aided in paleoenvironmental reconstructions. Micromammals (rodents and insectivores), as well as amphibians and insects, are paleoecologically sensitive. Comparisons of modern habitat and range of species to late Pleistocene and Holocene assemblages and distributions reveal disharmonious associations (that is, the occurrence of present taxa with separate geographic ranges that are presumed to be ecologically incompatible), especially in late Pleistocene assemblages. Tentative conclusions from micromammals and other environmental indicators suggest that the late Pleistocene supported an environment in which there coexisted plants and animals that are today separated by hundreds to thousands of kilometres (or considerable elevation differences). Stated in another way, the late Pleistocene climate was more equable than that of the present day, one in which seasonal extremes in temperature and effective moisture were reduced. The evolution of a modern biotic community, as opposed to one of the late Pleistocene, appears to be the consequence of intricate biological and biophysical interactions among individual species. Some researchers have theorized that the environmental changes that led to the formation of new biotic communities at the end of the Pleistocene resulted in the extinction of many of the Pleistocene faunal forms.

HOLOCENE CLIMATIC TRENDS AND CHRONOLOGY

In the mid-latitudes and the tropics, the end of the last glacial period was marked by a tremendous increase in rainfall. The increased precipitation toward the end of the Pleistocene was marked by a vast proliferation of pluvial lakes in the Great Basin of western North America, notably Lake Bonneville and Lake Lahontan (enormous ancestors of present-day Great Salt Lake and Pyramid Lake). Two peaks of lake levels were reached at about 12,000 ± 500 BP (the beginning of the Allerød Warm stage) and approximately 9000 ± 500 BP (the early Boreal Warm stage). At Lake Balaton (in Hungary) high terrace levels also mark the Allerød and early Boreal Warm stages. Lake Victoria (in East Africa) exhibits the identical twin oscillation in its terrace levels.

In equatorial regions the same evidence of high solar radiation and high rainfall at the end of the Pleistocene and during the early Holocene is apparent in the record of the Nile sediments. The Nile, like the other great rivers of Africa (notably, the Congo, Niger, and Sénégal), became quite reduced, if not totally blocked, by silt and desert sand during the low-precipitation, arid phases of the Pleistocene. An erroneous correlation between glacial phases and pluvial phases in the tropics has been widely accepted in the past, but cold ocean water means less precipitation, not more. The pluvial phases correspond to the high solar radiation states, the last maximum being about 10,000 years ago. Thus tremendous increases of Nile discharge are determined, by radiocarbon dating, to have occurred about 12,000 and 9,000 years ago, separated and followed by alluviation, indicating reduced runoff in the headwaters.

The expansion of monsoonal rains during the early Holocene in the tropical latitudes permitted an extensive spread of moist savanna-type vegetation over the Sahara in North Africa and the Kalahari in South Africa and in broad areas of Brazil, India, and Australia. Most of these areas had been dry savanna or arid during the last glacial period. Signs of late Paleolithic and Neolithic people can be seen throughout the Sahara today, and art is representative of the life and hunting scenes of the time. Lake deposits have been dated as young as 5000–6000 BP. Lake Chad covered a vast area in the very late Pleistocene and up to 5000 BP. Throughout the early Holocene, the Dead Sea shows a record of sedimentation from humid headwaters, and there was a Neolithic settlement at Jericho about 9000–10,000 BP.

In the high to mid-latitudes after the early Holocene, with its remnants of ice age conditions (tundra passing to birch forests), there was a transition to the mid-Holocene, marked by a progressive change to pine forest and then oak, beech, or mixed forest. The mean annual temperature reached 2.5°C (4.5°F) above that of today. Neolithic humans pressed forward across Europe and Asia. In the Canadian Arctic and in Manitoba the mean temperature passed 4°C (7.2°F) above present averages. It was a "milk-and-honey" period for early humans over much of the world, and in Europe it paved the way for the cultured races of the Bronze Age. Navigators started using the seaways to trade between the eastern Mediterranean, the British Isles, and the Baltic.

In the mid-latitude continental interiors there was still evidence of hot summers, but the winters were becoming colder and partly drier. There was an expansion of steppe or prairie conditions and their associated fauna and flora. Many lake levels showed a fall.

In Europe there was also the beginning of widespread deforestation as Bronze Age human communities started to use charcoal for smelting and extended agriculture to tilling and planting. As a consequence, soil erosion began almost immediately, hillsides developed lynchets (terracettes), and "anthropogenic sediments" began to accumulate on the lower floodplains.

At the corresponding latitudes in the Southern Hemisphere (approximately 30° to 35°S), pollen analysis indicates increasing desiccation during the Subboreal stage, with a maximum dryness about 3200 BP.

In the subtropical regions of Mesopotamia and the Nile valley, people had learned to harness water. The stationary settlements, advanced agriculture, and mild climates favoured a great flowering of human culture. It is surmised that, when the normal floods began to fail, human ingenuity rose to the occasion, as attested to by the development of irrigation canals and machinery.

The Sub-Atlantic stage (2200–0 BP) is the last major physical division of the geologic record. Historically, its beginning coincides with the rise of the Roman Empire in Europe, the flowering of the classical dynasties of China, the Ptolemies in Egypt, the Olmec of central Mexico and Guatemala, and the pre-Incan Chavín cultures of Peru.

The record of solar activity is disclosed by documentation of auroras in ancient Chinese court records and later by sunspot numbers. Both phenomena reflect solar activity in general, but correlation with weather records in the higher latitudes is complicated. Other indicators of climate, such as tree-ring analysis and palynology, were previously mentioned, but many documentary indications are also useful: the time of the cherry blossom festival in Kyōto, Japan, the freezing of lakes, the incidence of floods, blizzards, or droughts, the economics of harvests, salt evaporation production, some disease statistics, and so on. The water levels of closed basins such as the Caspian Sea and particularly the evaporite basin of the Kara-Bogaz-Gol Gulf reflect runoff to the Volga. The Dead Sea bears witness to eastern Mediterranean precipitation.

THE CLASSICAL ROMAN PERIOD

The Classical Roman Period is marked by the Florida or Roman emergence in the eustatic record about the BCE–CE boundary and succeeded by a transgression. The solar record is incomplete, but indications are for low activity. Records of rainfall kept by the astronomer Ptolemy (fl. 127–145 CE) in Alexandria noted thunderstorm activity in every summer month, in comparison with the totally dry summer today, which suggests a slightly wetter overall pattern in this latitude. In northern Europe and in other high latitudes, in contrast, the cool stage at the beginning of the 1st century CE may have been drier and more continental, as evidenced by dune building.

THE LATE ROMAN PERIOD

After the 1st century CE there is evidence of a progressive rise in sea level. Roman buildings and peat layers were covered by the marine transgression in the Netherlands, southern England, and parts of the Mediterranean. At the same time, drying and warming trends were associated with alluviation of streams and general desiccation in southern Europe and North Africa. Similar alluviation occurred in the American Southwest. This warming and desiccation trend is evident also in the subtropics of the Southern Hemisphere. The solar activity record indicates a mean intensity comparable to that of the mid-20th century.

THE POST-ROMAN AND CAROLINGIAN PERIOD

The Post-Roman and Carolingian Period extends roughly from 400 to 1000 CE. The important invasions of western Europe by the Huns and the Goths may have been generated by deteriorating climatic conditions in central Asia. Radiocarbon dating and studies of the ancient Chinese literature have disclosed that, when the glaciers of central Asia were large; the meltwaters fed springs, rivers, and lakes on the edge of the desert; and human communities flourished. When there was a warm phase, the water supply failed and the deserts encroached. Thus, in central Asia (and the Tarim Basin) during the cool Roman Period, the Old Silk Road permitted a regular trade between Rome and China, where the Han dynasty was flourishing. During the Ch'in, Wei, and Chou dynasties this trade declined. During the T'ang dynasty (618–907 CE) there was a reopening of the trade routes, and likewise during the Yüan dynasty (1206–1368). Marco Polo passed this way in 1271. Radiocarbon dates of the 8.6-metre-high (28 feet) lake level at Sogo Nur showed overflow conditions from 1300 to 1450, after which gradual, fluctuating, but progressive desiccation followed, and today the area is almost total desert.

In North America the Post-Roman and Carolingian Period was marked by warm temperatures in the northern parts, with mean paleotemperatures in central Canada about 1°C (1.8°F) more than the present. In the semiarid southwestern United States, the arroyos, washes, and ephemeral river valleys were filling slowly with alluvium (younger "Tsegi alluvium"), an indication that stream energy was generated by the summer flash floods. There were marginal retreats in almost all the mountain glacier regions of the world from the Alps to Patagonia.

In the tropical region of Central America there was the unexplained decline of the coastal Mayan people (Mexico and Guatemala) about the 10th century. The mountain Mayas continued to flourish, however, and it is possible that the high precipitation of this warming period introduced critical ecological limits to continued occupation of the (now) swampy coastal jungles.

THE VIKING-NORMAN PERIOD

Approximately 1000–1250 CE the worldwide warm-up that culminated in the 10th century and has been called the early Medieval Warm Period or the "Little Climatic Optimum," continued for two more centuries, but there was a brief drop in mean solar activity in the period about 1030–70. During the 8th to 10th centuries, the Vikings had extended as far afield as the Crimea and exploited coastal salt pans, the existence of which speak for seasonally high evaporation conditions and eustatic stability.

Widespread navigation by the Vikings occured in the Arctic regions during the 10th, 11th, and 12th centuries. Partly in response to reduced sea-ice conditions and milder climates they were able to establish settlements in

Iceland, southern Greenland (Erik the Red, c. 985), and in eastern North America (Vinland; Leif Eriksson, c. 1000). In Alaska, from tree-ring evidence, the mean temperature was 2 to 3°C (3.6 to 5.4°F) warmer in the 11th century than today. Eskimos had settled in Ellesmere Island about 900. Records of sea ice off Iceland show negligible severity from 865 to 1200, suggesting that often the westerly storm tracks must have passed north of Europe altogether.

After a brief interval of cold winters in Japan, the cherry blossoms returned to early blooming in the 12th century. In the semiarid southwestern United States there appears to have been increased precipitation, leading to a spread of vegetation and agriculture. Pueblo campsites dated 1100–1200 are found on top of the youngest Tsegi Alluvium. The snow line in the Rocky Mountains was about 300 metres (984 feet) higher than today, and similar trends are recorded in the Southern Hemisphere, notably in Australia and Chile. The first immigration of Maori peoples into New Zealand probably occurred at this mild time.

The Medieval Cool Period

The Medieval Cool Period, extending roughly from 1250 to 1500, corresponds to the Paria Emergence in the eustatic record and has been called one of the "little ice ages" by certain authors. Solar activity records show a decline from 1250 to 1350, a brief rise from 1350 to 1380, and then a phenomenal low that lasted until 1500. Pollen records in northern Europe reveal rather consistently cool conditions, and smoothed mean temperature curves show a cumulative drop during this period. Stalactite studies in a karst cave in France showed a travertine growth peak (indicating cool, moist conditions) in 1450. In North America these cool, moist conditions were widespread at first, but became dry later. The arroyos and washes filled with the Naha Alluvium, and the human population decreased markedly. There is pollen evidence of a temperature drop of about 1°C (1.8°F). This is the period of the "Great Drought." In the upper Mississippi valley the Indian cultures began a general decline, accompanied by a transfer from agriculture to hunting. It was similar in the western prairies, and it was this hunting culture that the first Spanish explorers encountered.

In the Canadian north the mean temperatures had dropped about 2°C (3.6°F) below the previous high. In the Sierra Nevada, the Rockies, and Alaska there were glacial readvances, with evidence of a 2°C (3.6°F) temperature drop. In the Arctic regions, the Eskimo economy underwent a marked change to adjust to these more extreme conditions, which amounted to about 5 to 6°C (9 to 10.8°F) less than the mean of the climatic optimum.

The Norse settlements in Greenland were abandoned altogether as the permafrost advanced. Pollen studies at Godthåb indicate a shift from a maritime climate to a cold, dry continental regime. The sea ice off Iceland reveals an extraordinary growth in severity, from zero coverage before the year 1200 to eight-week average cover in the 13th century, rising to 40 weeks in the 19th century, and dropping again to eight weeks in the 20th century. In Japan there were glacial readvances and a mean winter temperature drop of 3.5°C (6.3°F). Summers were marked by excessive rains and bad harvests.

The equatorial regions now began a marked desiccation, with a drop in level of all the great African lakes. The Nile suffered a decreased flow and alluviation. South of the equator in the temperate belts there occurred a general return to cooler and wetter conditions that have continued (with oscillations) until the present time in southern Chile, Patagonia, southernmost Africa, south-western Australia, and New Zealand.

THE LITTLE ICE AGE

Throughout most of what is commonly called the Little Ice Age (1500–1850) the mean solar activity was quite low, but positive fluctuations occurred about 1540–90 and 1770–1800. The main westerly storm belts shifted about 500 km (310 miles) to the south, and for much of the time the northern latitudes came under cool continental conditions. Observed temperature series in Europe from Paris to Leningrad show large fluctuations until 1850.

Glacier advances are recorded in the Alps, in the Sierra Nevada, and in Alaska. Corresponding low sea levels are recorded by early tide gauge records in the Netherlands and Germany. Even in equatorial latitudes there are traces of mountain glacier advances (as in the Andes of Colombia).

THE ANTHROPOCENE EPOCH

The Anthropocene Epoch is an unofficial interval of geologic time characterized by the release of greenhouse gases into the atmosphere resulting from the onset of organized human industrial activity. Although the modern period of Earth's history is conventionally defined as residing within the Holocene Epoch (11,700 years ago to the present), some scientists argue that the Holocene terminated in the relatively recent past. They contend that Earth currently resides in a climatic interval during which humans have exerted a dominant influence over climate. The onset of the Anthropocene Epoch, so-named by Dutch chemist Paul Crutzen, is said to be coincident with the creation of the steam engine by Scottish inventor James Watt in 1784.

Increased industrialization in the 19th century brought forth large-scale deforestation and soil erosion. Thomas D. McAvoy/Time & Life Pictures/ Getty Images

THE INDUSTRIAL AGE (1850–1950)

The year 1850 started a brief warming trend that persisted for 100 years. It also approximates a critical turning point in climatic, sea level, glacial, and sedimentologic records.

In many regions of central and southern Europe "anthro-pogenic" sediments (or cultural layers) began to appear in Neolithic times (early to mid-Holocene). Elsewhere in the world (such as in North America, Australia, South Africa), however, this type of sedimentation began about the middle of the 19th century, depending on soil erosion stimulated by mechanized (disk) plowing, large-scale deforestation, and engineering activity. Thus, independently of natural climatic change, the century 1850–1950, marked by anthropogenic aridification, proved to be a time of man-made deserts.

CHAPTER 8

THE CENOZOIC AND BEYOND

In just 66 million years, the reins of power shifted from large, ferocious ruling reptiles to small, fragile, bipedal mammals. Like the dinosaurs that preceded them, mammals seized the opportunities provided by an extinction event that wiped out their competition at the end of the previous era. They diversified and spread across the globe. Some mammalian forms existed for a time and died out, whereas others became the ancestors of the familiar lineages known today. The members of one of these lineages, a primate genus called *Homo*, became increasingly capable of altering the world around them. Throughout the most recent 10,000 years, human beings (members of the species *Homo sapiens sapiens*) have changed the courses of rivers, transformed landscapes, and caused the extinction of many other species. Such human-induced extinctions have increased significantly over the last 100 years. It is important to remember that the time of the dinosaurs was bounded by great extinction events. Time will tell whether the same fate will befall the mammals of the Cenozoic.

GLOSSARY

albedo The fraction of light reflected by a body or surface.

australopithecines The first creatures that can be described as human.

biostratigraphic units Bodies of rocks characterized by specific fossil assemblages.

chronostratigraphic units Bodies of rocks deposited during a distinct interval of time.

catarrhines Old World monkeys, apes, and humans that have narrow noses and truly opposable thumbs.

Cretaceous–Tertiary (K–T) extinction Global extinction event that eliminated approximately 80% of all species of animals, including most dinosaurs and many marine invertebrates.

diatoms Any of a class of infinitesimal, planktonic, unicellular or colonial algae with silicified cell walls.

drumlin An oval or elongated hill thought to result from the streamlined movement of glacial ice sheets across rock debris, or till.

esker A long, narrow, winding ridge composed of stratified sand and gravel deposited by a subglacial or englacial meltwater stream.

fjord A long narrow arm of the sea, commonly extending far inland, that results from marine inundation of a glaciated valley.

greenhouse effect The trapping of heat (infrared radiation) from the Sun and re-emitted by Earth's surface in the lower levels of the atmosphere by carbon dioxide, water vapour, and certain other gases.

ice age Geologic interval during which thick ice sheets cover vast areas of land.

igneous rock Any of various crystalline or glassy rocks formed by the cooling and solidification of molten earth material.

lee The side that is sheltered from the wind.

loess Deposits of windblown dust and silt.

marl Old term used to refer to an earthy mixture of fine-grained minerals. The term was applied to a variety of sediments and rocks with a considerable range of composition.

Meissner's corpuscles Principal receptors for touch in hairless skin, which helped primates adapt to treelike environments and grasslands.

metamorphism Mineralogical and structural adjustments of solid rocks to physical and chemical conditions differing from those under which the rocks originally formed.

moraine Accumulation of rock debris (till) carried or deposited by a glacier.

nannofossil Ocean-dwelling golden-brown algal remains.

obsidian A black, glassy rock of volcanic origin that can be used for dating.

psychrosphere The deep, dense, permanently cold layer of the ocean.

platyrrhines Broad-nosed New World monkeys.

sapropel A loose sedimentary deposit rich in bituminous material.

stoss The side of a rock face oriented toward the direction from which an overriding glacier impinges.

Thulean Land Bridge Continental connection that allowed terrestrial mammals to cross between western Eurasia and eastern North America.

till Unsorted material laid down directly or reworked by a glacier.

FOR FURTHER READING

Agusta, Jordi, and Mauricio Anton. *Mammoths, Sabertooths, and Hominids: 65 Million Years of Mammalian Evolution in Europe*. Columbia University Press: New York, NY: 2002.

Bloom, Arthur L. *Geomorphology: A Systematic Analysis of Late Cenozoic Landforms*, 3rd ed. Upper Saddle River, NJ: Prentice Hall, 2004.

Boggs, Sam, Jr. *Principles of Sedimentology and Stratigraphy*. Upper Saddle River, NJ: Prentice Hall, 2005.

Bonis, Louis de, George D. Koufos, and Peter Andrews. *Hominoid Evolution and Climatic Change in Europe: Volume 2: Phylogeny of the Neogene Hominoid Primates of Eurasia*. Cambridge, England: Cambridge University Press, 2001.

Brookfield, Michael E. *Principles of Stratigraphy*. Hoboken, NJ: Wiley, 2004.

Chernicoff, Stanley. *Geology*, 4th ed. Upper Saddle River, NJ: Prentice Hall, 2006.

Falkowski, Paul, Andrew H. Knoll, eds. *Evolution of Primary Producers in the Sea*. Burlington, MA: Elsevier, 2007.

Haines, Tim, and Paul Chambers. *The Complete Guide to Prehistoric Life*. Ontario, Canada: Firefly Books, 2006.

Mackay, Anson, Rick Battarbee, John Birks, and Frank Oldfield. *Global Change in the Holocene*. New York, NY: Oxford University Press, 2005.

Marshak, Stephen. *Essentials of Geology*, 3rd. ed. New York, NY: W.W. Norton, 2009.

Mayr, Gerald. *Paleogene Fossil Birds*. Frankfurt, Germany: Springer, 2009.

Nichols, Douglas J., and Kirk R. Johnson. *Plants and the K-T Boundary*. Cambridge, England: Cambridge University Press, 2008.

Parrish, Judith Totman. *Interpreting Pre-Quaternary Climate from the Geologic Record*. New York, NY: Columbia University Press, 2001.

Petuch, Edward J. *Cenozoic Seas: The View from Eastern North America*. Boca Raton, FL: CRC Press, 2004.

Prothero, Donald R. *Evolution: What the Fossils Say and Why It Matters*. New York: Columbia University Press, 2007.

Prothero, Donald R., Linda C. Ivany, and Elizabeth A. Nesbitt (eds.). *From Greenhouse to Icehouse: The Marine Eocene-Oligocene Transition*, New York, NY: Columbia University Press, 2003.

Rose, Kenneth D. *The Beginning of the Age of Mammals*. Baltimore, MD: Johns Hopkins University Press, 2006.

Siegert Martin J. *Ice Sheets and Late Quaternary Environmental Change*. West Sussex, England: John Wiley & Sons, 2001.

Stanley, Steven M. *Earth System History*, 2nd. ed. New York, NY: W. H. Freeman, 2004.

Tarbuck, Edward J., Dennis Tasa, and Frederick K. Lutgens. *Earth: An Introduction to Physical Geology*. Upper Saddle River, NJ: Prentice Hall, 2007.

Woodburne, Michael O., ed. *Late Cretaceous and Cenozoic Mammals of North America: Biostratigraphy and Geochronology*. New York, NY: Columbia University Press, 2004.

INDEX

sea level changes, 137–139, 150,
  152, 186, 188–189, 193,
  207–208, 209, 210–211, 214,
  215, 224, 228
Selandian Stage, 73
Serravallian Stage, 104, 108–109
Simons, Elwyn, 123
Sivapithecus, 125–126

T

taeniodonts, 101–102
Tarantian Stage, 175, 177–178
tectonic subsidence/uplift,
  213–214, 215–216
Tertiary deposits, occurrence
  and distribution of, 58–66
  sedimentary sequences, 63–66
  volcanism and orogenesis,
    59–63
Tertiary Period, 30–72, 73, 104,
  128
  correlation of strata, 70–72
  environment of, 31–42
  establishing boundaries of,
    66–69, 70
  life during, 42–55
  paleoclimate, 38–42
  paleogeography, 32–38
  rocks of, 55–72
  subdivisions of, 30, 56–58, 67

Thanetian Stage, 73, 80
Thylacosmilus, 126
titanothere, 102
Tortonian Stage, 104, 109–110
Toxodon, 161–162

U

Uintatherium, 103

V

Venericardia, 103
Viking-Norman Period, 225–226
Vrba, Elisabeth, 144

W

Wilson, Allan, 123–124
woolly rhinoceros, 141, 162, 193

Y

Ypresian Stage, 77, 80

Z

Zanclean Stage, 110, 112–113